CÁNTARO **Cá**²⁰ LIBRARY

A TREATISE

TO CONFIRM THE CHRISTIAN FAITH OF THE BARBARY CAPTIVES

CIPRIANO DE VALERA

Foreword and Translation by Steven R. Martins

Dedicated to my faithful brother in the faith,
J.D. Fasolino

cántaro
publications

cantaroinstitute.org

A Treatise to Confirm the Christian Faith of the Barbary Captives
Published by Cántaro Publications, a publishing imprint of
Cántaro Institute, Jordan Station, ON.

*Un Tratado para confirmar en la fe cristiana a los cautivos de
berberia* by Cipriano de Valera, originally published 1594.

Translation by Steven R. Martins

Proofread Editor: Russell Galloway

ISBN: 978-1-990771-44-6

Printed in the United States of America

CONTENTS

FOREWORD

S INCE THE 500th anniversary of the protestant reformation, there has been renewed interest in recovering and recounting the history and heritage of the reformation. One particular area that has been given some attention as of late—*long overdue attention*—has been the reformation in Spain, or to put it more accurately, the reformation that began in Spain but which was later expatriated due to the growing threat of Inquisitorial persecution. It pains me to say that to this day, many of the works of the Spanish reformers remain untranslated. In some cases, they still remain in their sixteenth-century form of writing; in most cases, they have been translated to a nineteenth-century form of Spanish; and very few have been translated into modern English and Spanish. Out of much of the forgotten works by these forgotten Spanish reformers, those perhaps most unjustly forgotten, considering the magnitude of their significance, are that of Cipriano de Valera (c. 1532-1602), who is very much a giant in the land of the reformers.

A Forgotten Reformer

Valera was born in c. 1532 at Fregenal de la Sierra, Badajoz, and in adulthood spent approximately six years at the university of his hometown in Seville. He is recorded to have studied dialectics and philosophy, graduating with a bachelor's degree that would be recognized outside of Spain.[1] In his early twenties, he became a member of the Order of Observantine Hieronymites in the monastery of San Isidoro del Campo, which laid a few miles northwest of his hometown of Seville.[2] If the Inquisition had not

---

1. A. Gordon Kinder, "Religious Literature as an Offensive Weapon: Cipriano de Valera's Part in England's War with Spain", *The Sixteenth Century Journal: The Journal of Early Modern Studies*, Vol. 19, No. 2 (Summer, 1988), 223.

2. Bibliotheca Wiffeniana, *Spanish Reformers of Two Centuries from 1520: Their Lives and Writings, According to the late Benjamin B. Wiffen's Plan and with the Use of His Materials. Described by Edward Boehmer* (Strassburg, 1904), Vol. III, 149.; Kinder, "Religious Literature as an Offensive Weapon", 223.

had its way, one could argue that the reformation movement that was preparing to sweep through Spain would have had such a profound cultural impact given the primary base from which the movement would have sprung. Historian Lewis J. Hutton writes that, given the role of the Hieronymite Order in "giving expression to a distinctive Spanish spirituality", Spain could have well "achieved an industrial technology and a European type of capitalism", a thesis originally put forward by Américo Castro in his book *Aspectos del Vivir Hispánico*, an expansion of Marcel Bataillon's *Erasme et l'Espagne*.[3] This had something to do with "manual work" being seen and treated as a "renascence of the initial program of the Franciscans... a characteristic of those who first followed the Hieronymite expression of the religious life,"[4] and which summed up could be expressed, though in a raw and undeveloped form, as worshiping God in all aspects of life, and not solely perceived as within the confines of that which was supposedly "sacred" as per medieval scholastic thought. To put it differently,

---

3.   Lewis J. Hutton, "The Spanish Heretic: Cipriano de Valera", *Church History*, Cambridge University Press, Vol. 27, No. 1 (March, 1958), 23.

4.   Ibid., 24.

we might say that the Order of Observantine Hieronymites had the embers of what would later become the "protestant work ethic",[5] but in contrast to other places in Europe which saw this development and flourishment, such embers were snuffed out by the Inquisition.

The brothers of this particular monastery are said to have been deeply influenced by the protestant reformation in the 1550s, being exposed to the works from Germany (Martin Luther) and Geneva (John Calvin),[6] and it was not until 1557 that the Spanish religious authorities became aware of this growing protestant community and unleashed the Inquisition in swift

---

5. "The pioneering sociologist Max Weber was the first to draw attention to the Protestant work ethic. In his book *The Protestant Ethic and the Spirit of Capitalism*, published in 1904, [he] studied the phenomenal economic growth, social mobility, and cultural change that accompanied the Reformation. He went so far as to credit the Reformation for the rise of capitalism", in Gene Edward Veith, "The Protestant Work Ethic", *Ligonier Ministries*. Accessed January 15, 2024, https://www.ligonier.org/learn/articles/protestant-work-ethic.

6. Hutton, "The Spanish Heretic: Cipriano de Valera", 25.

and deadly response.[7] Many were apprehended and suffered terribly, dying at the hands of their Catholic persecutors, but some few managed to escape and to find safe harbours that provided a more congenial theological climate for protestant convictions. Valera was one of those who managed to escape.[8] It is thanks to the *Artes de la Inquisizion Española* (1567) that we have such information regarding how this transpired, from the infiltration of reformed ideas to the springing of the Inquisition, a work which was authored by the pseudonym Raimundo Gonzalez de Montes, some of which have claimed was the pseudonym for Casiodoro de Reina or Antonio del Coro.[9]

Valera is believed to have travelled to Geneva with a few of his Spanish protestant brothers,[10] and while his time with John Calvin (which is

---

7. Kinder, "Religious Literature as an Offensive Weapon: Cipriano de Valera's Part in England's War with Spain", 223.

8. Ibid., 223.

9. Hutton, 25.

10. Natalio Ohanna, "Heterodoxos en cautiverio: de Cipriano de Valera a los protestantes del norte de África", *Hispanic Review*, University of Pennsylvania Press, Vol. 80, No. 1, (Winter, 2012), 22.

assumed given his later Spanish translation of *The Institutes of the Christian Religion*, which was Calvin's *magnum opus*) proved to be influential for his own theological development, leading him to become a doctrinal Calvinist, he did not remain in Geneva due to the tragic fate of Servetus, who was killed for his unitarian, heretical views. While Valera was Trinitarian in his doctrinal understanding of God, he was Spanish like Servetus, and given the suspicions that arose concerning Casiodoro de Reina's friendship with Servetus—Reina being a mentor of Valera since their time at the monastery in Seville—it became clear that Calvin did not "take kindly to Spaniards."[11] This led to Valera's departure from Geneva, and with the rise of Queen Elizabeth in England, he was amongst many Spanish refugees who made their way to protestant lands, arriving in London in 1558.[12] As Valera states in his introduction to the *Instituzion Relijiosa*:

> Thousands and thousands of poor strangers have taken themselves to England (I do not mention

---

11. Kinder, "Religious Literature as an Offensive Weapon: Cipriano de Valera's Part in England's War with Spain", 224.

12. Ibid.

other Kingdoms and Republics) to save their consciences and their lives, where, under the protection and care, first of God and after of the most serene lady, Queen Elizabeth, they have been defended and cared for against the tyranny of the Antichrist and his sons the Inquisitors.[13]

While Reina would go on to plant and pastor a church in London, "under the aegis of the so-called *coetus*, or council, of the Strangers' Churches", Valera went instead to Cambridge, where his degree from Seville was recognized and where he was incorporated by the University on February 9, 1559.[14] On January 12 of the following year, "he was appointed to a fellowship of Magdalene College in that university, where his distinguished countryman, Francisco de Enzinas (Dryander), had also served"[15] prior to the Marian

---

13. Cipriano de Valera, "A Todos los Fieles de la Nazion Española", in Juan Calvino, *Instituzion Relijiosa* (1536), traduzida al castellano por Cipriano de Valera en 1597. Vol. XIV of *Reformistas Antiguos Españoles* edited by Luis Usoz y Rio (Madrid, 1858), 9.

14. Kinder, "Religious Literature as an Offensive Weapon: Cipriano de Valera's Part in England's War with Spain", 224.

15. Ibid.

persecution.[16] We do not have presently available evidence to determine what exactly Valera taught while at Cambridge, but we can assume that given the English were seeking to fortify their protestant position, and given that there were quite a number of foreign protestants at Oxford and Cambridge in teaching positions, that Valera likely was a professor of theology.[17] What we do know for certain is that he remained in his post until 1567.[18] After this Valera moved to London, the city where Reina had been pastoring, and due to Reina's quick departure from England, orchestrated by the spies and agents of the Inquisition by means of a false scandal, it is believed that Valera took on the pastoral position of the Spanish church until its eventual dissolution, after which

---

16. During her five-year reign, Queen Mary of England (1516-1558) had over 300 religious dissenters burned at the stake in what are known as the Marian persecutions.

17. Ivan E. Mesa, "'Open Your Eyes, O Spaniards': Cipriano de Valera — A Forgotten Spanish Protestant of the 16th Century", *The Banner of Truth* (Feb. 2015), 25.

18. Kinder, "Religious Literature as an Offensive Weapon: Cipriano de Valera's Part in England's War with Spain", 224.

Valera then attended the Italian congregation.[19] Valera, by this time, was married and had several children. It could well be said that Valera not only found a place to do ministry as a protestant, both for those within England and for those Spaniards

19. Ibid., 225.; While Kinder believes that the Spanish church dissolved immediately after Reina's departure, it is difficult to assume this given that Valera was just as invested in this Spanish church as Reina. While not a member in residence of the church while in Cambridge, he nonetheless contributed to *The Spanish Confession of the Christian Faith* presented by Reina by editing the work prior to its submission to the consistories and its publication. See *The Spanish Confession of the Christian Faith* (Jordan Station, ON., Cántaro Publications, 2023). Perhaps the Spanish church eventually dissolved given the absence of its founding pastor; I believe it is premature to suggest that it dissolved immediately and did not at least dissolve gradually under the leadership of Valera who served as a minister of the Church of St. Mary Axe, which housed the Spanish congregation of protestant refugees. But Hutton claims otherwise, he claims that the Spanish church continued to meet under Valera's pastoral leadership, and we have no reason to conclude that the church dissolved while he remained in his post. See Hutton, "The Spanish Heretic", 27.

exiled and held captive due to their protestant convictions, but also found a place to call home.

In the Spanish Armada year, which was 1588, that time when the Spanish armada cataclysmically failed to invade England, Valera began to ramp up his written compositions of Spanish protestant literature in hopes of (1) fortifying the propaganda against Catholic Spain, and (2) edifying protestants within Spain who were in the clutches of the Inquisition as well as those who were exiled from their motherland.[20] We know this not only because of the historical and cultural context at the time, but because Valera also admitted that his literary attempts to make the Word of God available was an "effective weapon against Antichrist in Spain."[21] This, and the fact

---

20. Kinder, "Religious Literature as an Offensive Weapon: Cipriano de Valera's Part in England's War with Spain", 223, 225.

21. Valera in the preface to *Catholico Reformado*, A4r: "Lo qual espero en mi Dios que con este y otros semejantes libros en que se trata la palabra de Dios, vendrá algún día en efecto. Porque los verdaderos soldados, las verdaderas lanças, espadas, arcabuzes, mosquetas y lombardas para hazer la guerra al Antechristo es la palabra de Dios: con esta palabra el Antechristo ha recibido mortales heridas: de las quales sin duda morira."

that we find another who also contributed to the Spanish literary production, his former companion Antonio del Corro, another Spanish reformer.[22] We can only imagine how gleeful the English were to have Valera in their ranks, as he would demonstrate to not only teach well, but to have the capacity of "writing religious polemic", becoming a "very desirable asset to the English in this ideological contest" of protestant truth over Catholic error. Of out his many contributions, Valera's *Dos Tratados del Papa y de la Misa*, or *The Two Treatises on the Pope and Mass*, was one of the most formidable, which, according to Spanish reformation scholar Gordon A. Kinder, "has the distinction of being the first original edition of a Spanish work and only the second book in Spanish to be printed in England."[23] The general thrust of this work was to inform the reader Scriptural truth in such a way that it invalidated

---

22. Kinder, "Religious Literature as an Offensive Weapon: Cipriano de Valera's Part in England's War with Spain", 225.

23. Ibid., 226.; Kinder also notes that the first Spanish book to be printed in England was Corro's *Reglas gramaticales para aprender la lengua española y francesa*, published in Oxford by Joseph Barnes, 1586.

the claims of the papacy and therefore the papacy itself while at the same time exposing many elements of the Catholic mass as being syncretistic and pagan in nature, accomplishing its objective of demolishing both these mainstays of Roman Catholicism. As Kinder notes, "demolish either and the other will fall with it."[24]

The other most notable contribution is his *Tratado para confirmar en la fe Cristiana a los cautivos de Berberia*, which when translated can be rendered as *A Treatise to Confirm the Christian Faith of the Barbary Captives.* This work, which is the occasion of this extensive foreword, was printed by Peter Short in 1594 as a "106-page octavo book, to which was [originally] appended the first edition of *Enxambre de los falsos milagros*."[25] For those unfamiliar with the term Barbary within this context, it is in reference to the Barbary pirates, or corsairs.[26] The Barbary were essentially

24. Kinder, "Religious Literature as an Offensive Weapon: Cipriano de Valera's Part in England's War with Spain", 227.

25. Ibid., 230.

26. See Hugh Murray, *The Encyclopaedia of Geography: Comprising a Complete Description of the Earth, Physical, Statistical, Civil and Political* (Lea and Blanchard, 1841).

Muslim pirates operating from the coast of North Africa. They peaked in their power during the seventeenth century and remained in activity well into the nineteenth century. While piracy can be generally reduced to rogue agents operating on the sea for their own monetary gain, the Barbary were of political importance ever since the sixteenth century given the accomplishments and directives of Barbarossa (Khayr al-Din) who united Algeria and Tunisia under the Ottoman sultanate and secured through the means of piracy a steady revenue.[27] Their primary objective was the capture of slaves for the Islamic slave trade, and these slaves often consisted of Christians and Jews, and in some cases, fellow Muslims as well.[28] Spain and Portugal knew the Barbary pirates, or corsairs, well because the Barbary notoriously raided coastal towns and villages, to such an extent that it became difficult to settle such coastal regions. Valera's treatise, thus understood

---

27. Ohanna, "Heterodoxos en cautiverio: de Cipriano de Valera a los protestantes del norte de África", 23.

28. Robert Davis, "British Slaves on the Barbary Coast", *BBC*. Accessed January 08, 2024, https://www.bbc.co.uk/history/british/empire_seapower/white_slaves_01.shtml/.

within this historical context, can be understood as a letter to all those protestants who came to saving faith either before or during their captivity under the Ottomans. The treatise had been written from a burdened and pastoral heart to particularly "encourage captives of the Barbary pirates who were galley-slaves."[29] While an argument has been made within scholarship that what Valera meant by "Barbary" was actually Spain and its Inquisitorial agents, and the "captives" were those protestants in dungeons facing the charges of the Inquisition,[30] the clear reference to Moors in the body of the work makes it clear that Valera had in mind those poor captives at the hands of the Muslims.[31] The possibility certainly remains open for what scholarship currently suggests, but no argument can be set forth that it is either one or the other, why not both if there remains such insistence? Valera was explicit enough in his writing to make clear his primary readership. And so

29. Kinder, "Religious Literature as an Offensive Weapon: Cipriano de Valera's Part in England's War with Spain", 230.

30. Ibid.

31. Ohanna, "Heterodoxos en cautiverio: de Cipriano de Valera a los protestantes del norte de África", 31.

well written was this treatise that centuries later, the Catholic historian Marcelino Menéndez y Pelayo, who had a consistent disdain for the Spanish protestants,[32] remarked that Valera's treatise was written with remarkable fervor and eloquence.[33]

Valera produced many other works, including *Aviso sobre los Jubileos*, or *Warning about Jubilees*, and the Spanish translation of Calvin's *Institutes of the Christian Religion*, but what he is most well known for is his editorial work on the revised Spanish translation of the Bible, which has been referred to as the *Biblia del Cántaro*.[34]

It is worth mentioning that though Valera remained in safe harbours while producing all of his work, he was nonetheless tried in absentia, and found guilty of heresy by the Inquisition. His effigy was later burned at the stake after its presentation in the *auto-da-fé* in Sevilla on April

---

32. Hutton, "The Spanish Heretic: Cipriano de Valera", 30.

33. Marcelino Menéndez y Pelayo, *Historia de los Heterodoxos*, 5:186-189.

34. Kinder, "Religious Literature as an Offensive Weapon: Cipriano de Valera's Part in England's War with Spain", 233.

26, 1562.[35] Not at all surprising, given that he was considered the chief Spanish heretic by the Spanish Inquisition.[36] Such a formidable foe was Valera, that all his literary contributions were like dynamic artillery fire. As Hutton writes, Valera was the protestant heretic, in the eyes of the Inquisition, *"par excellence."*[37] And what was it that made him such a threat to Catholic Spain? His reformation spirit. As Ivan Mesa writes:

> In his most anti-papal remarks, Valera accused the Roman Catholic Church of having abandoned the path of the apostles and the commandment of Christ, for not caring for the sheep, and for suppressing them in ignorance. These leaders claimed to be 'vicars of Christ' but in reality they were guilty of pulling people away from a true knowledge of and obedience to

---

35. Madrid, Archivo Histórico Nacional, Inq. leg. 20721, fol. 8v: "Fray Cipriano, frayle del dicho monasterio absente condenado, relaxado su estatua por herege lutherano."

36. Mesa, "'Open Your Eyes, O Spaniards': Cipriano de Valera — A Forgotten Spanish Protestant of the 16th Century", 26.

37. Hutton, "The Spanish Heretic: Cipriano de Valera", 24.

Christ. Valera sounded a clear warning against false teachers...[38]

In retrospect, as one considers the contributions of Valera,[39] although minor in comparison to the other reformers of his time, he is nevertheless a giant amongst the Spanish reformers, well trained in his theology, Calvinistic in doctrine,[40] well versed in the writings of the patristics and in the history of the church. Demonstrating such wide breadth of knowledge, including "the lives of the saints, medieval theologians, Roman Catholic writers, particularly Spanish and Italian" and acquainted with "classical pagan authors and Italian and Spanish secular poets... and a wide variety of Protestant works" and ancient Jewish documents—referencing, for example, Josephus' *Fall of Jerusalem* in his treatise to the Barbary

---

38. Mesa, "'Open Your Eyes, O Spaniards': Cipriano de Valera — A Forgotten Spanish Protestant of the 16th Century", 27.

39. Hutton, "The Spanish Heretic: Cipriano de Valera", 28.

40. See Thomas McCrie, *History of the Spanish Reformation: Progress & Suppression in the 16th Century* (Jordan Station, ON.: Cántaro Publications, 2023), 379.

captives—Valera is in every way a significant Spanish protestant scholar worthy of our consideration.[41] As Kinder writes:

> The great interest in Cipriano de Valera is that here was a Spaniard, born and brought up in Spain, who, so far as we know, had never traveled abroad, yet who nevertheless became a convinced and propagandizing Protestant, ready to leave home and endure permanent exile for the beliefs he held. He certainly tried to live by the quotation from I Esdras 4:38, "Vale y Valera la Verdad" (The truth abides and is strong for ever), which he used as a canting personal motto.[42]

Valera must be seen not only as a remarkable scholar, but also as a phenomenal apologist and evangelist. In truth, as one reads his many works and contributions to the expatriated Spanish

---

41. Kinder, "Religious Literature as an Offensive Weapon: Cipriano de Valera's Part in England's War with Spain", 228, 235.; See G. A. Kinder, "Three Spanish Reformers," 385-390.; Ohanna, "Heterodoxos en cautiverio: de Cipriano de Valera a los protestantes del norte de África", 26.

42. Kinder, "Religious Literature as an Offensive Weapon: Cipriano de Valera's Part in England's War with Spain", 235.

reformation, we see in Valera, not only a strong reformational spirit, but also an evangelistic zeal and pastoral concern, evidenced by his expression of sorrow and heaviness of heart for those faithful who are afflicted and for those who are lost in their sin. No one does the kind of things that Valera did unless they have an unquestionable conviction and a "burning desire" as we see expressed in Valera's own writing:

> Open your eyes, O Spaniards, and forsaking those who deceive you, obey Christ and His Word which alone is firm and unchangeable for ever. Establish and found your faith on the true foundation of the Prophets and Apostles and sole Head of His Church.[43]

A Gift to the Present Church

It is in light of this historical context that the Cántaro Institute is most honoured to bring Valera's work into both modern English and Spanish print. And in regards to the *Tratado para confirmar en la fe Cristiana a los cautivos de Berberia*, as far as our research team has been able to affirm, what you presently hold in your hands

---

43. Valera, "A Todos los Fieles de la Nazion Española", 12.

is the first English translation of Valera's work—or, at the very least, the first English translation made publicly available. It is our aim to continue to bring these forgotten works into the light, one after the other. As Mesa rightly identifies:

> In recent years there has been a growing interest in Reformed theology in the English-speaking world. While grateful for this trend, there is need for this same renewal among Spanish-speakers. A study of the sixteenth-century Spanish Protestants, including Cipriano de Valera, is a great source of encouragement as well as a reminder that the preaching of the gospel and Reformed truths have not been unknown in the Spanish language.[44]

We could not have put it any better. There is a need, and the Cántaro Institute seeks to meet that need. And not only for the Spanish-speaking world, but for the entirety of the Anglosphere as well, which has had insufficient exposure to such Spanish protestant works. What you have before you, *A Treatise to Confirm the Christian Faith of the Barbary Captives*, is truthfully a reformational

---

44. Mesa, "'Open Your Eyes, O Spaniards': Cipriano de Valera — A Forgotten Spanish Protestant of the 16th Century", 29.

jewel. As you carefully read through it, discerning and meditating on Valera's thought, you will find that, in comparison to much of the other works produced in the sixteenth century which reference the Moors and the Islamic people, Valera takes a less polemical and more missional approach, deconstructing not only Catholicism and Judaism, but also Islam as a descendent of that heretical branch of the Christian faith known as fourth century Arianism.[45] He also encourages gospel witness to these godless men and women, harbouring deep within the hope that those protestant, Christian captives might sow the seed of the gospel and witness it bear fruit amongst their captors.[46] Valera had the audacity to believe, as we all should, that the gospel can transform the hearts of those whom we might perceive as our most bitter enemies. That should provoke us to equal or greater faith in what the gospel can accomplish by the power of the Spirit of God.

Soli Deo Gloria.

---

45. Ohanna, "Heterodoxos en cautiverio: de Cipriano de Valera a los protestantes del norte de África", 27-28.

46. Ibid., 22, 35.

INTRODUCTION TO
THE 1872 EDITION

ALLOW THE WORDS OF Don Luis de
Usoz y Rio to serve as an introductory
note for this treatise. His contributions
to the nation of Spain have been substantial, no-
tably through his efforts in reprinting this and
numerous other works of early Spanish reformers. Without his intervention, these significant
texts might have languished in obscurity, lost to
posterity forever.

Truly, in the terrifying records of captivity and
slavery, and in the equally sad tales of the hardened and constant indifference of tyrants, there
is no more distressing and misery-laden specta-
cle than the life of captives in Barbary, especially
in the den of thieves of Algiers, which was visible and bordered the realms of our acclaimed
monarchs, Carlos I and Felipe II. There, fifty
thousand captives groaned in torment in Algiers

1

alone... and these sorrows, losses, and endless captivities, which were neither remedied nor ended by Lord Don Carlos I, only escalated under the governance of his wise, prudent, and astute son, Don Felipe II. Referring to him and these events, one of our historians, clad in black, exclaimed in these terms:

> "Isn't it a great shame for Christians that so many kings extravagantly waste treasures and profanely ruin wealth, yet when it comes to helping a Christian captive, they are stingy, harsh, greedy, and cowardly? Why can't they see that nothing would earn them more love and awe from the world than leading a procession of captives back to Spain? ... Therefore, Valera, understanding the captives' dire situation, did the only thing he could — offering them this kind of Consolatory Epistle, the ultimate and most effective solace for the sorrowful, the comfort of religion. In doing so, he followed in the footsteps of his countryman, Doctor Juan Perez, in a fitting and appropriate way, as the captives in Barbary needed the same encouragement and comfort as those suffering under the Inquisition...

I conclude by urging everyone who cares about Spain's wellbeing to read this work and the others I've managed to reprint with attention and good intention. They are all valuable symbols of Spanish identity, created in times that are often pointed to as the best in Spain's history by our contemporaries, who see themselves as true, learned, and noble Spaniards...

I will conclude by appealing to every friend of Spain's welfare to read this work and those previously reprinted, as well as those I have managed to reprint, with attentive and good intentions. All these works are valuable tokens of Spanish identity, created in times often recommended as Spain's best by our contemporaries, who are considered true, learned, and noble Spaniards."

"Yet for your sake we are killed all the day long;
we are regarded as sheep to be slaughtered.
Awake, why sleepest thou, O Lord? arise,
cast us not off for ever."

— Psalm 44:22-23

A TREATISE CONFIRMING THE CHRISTIAN FAITH OF THE BARBARY CAPTIVES

Cipriano de Valera

(1594)

To all the poor captives in Barbary, who suffer for the Gospel of Jesus Christ, greetings in the same Lord.

BELOVED BROTHERS IN THE LORD! Through very certain news, both spoken and written, I have come to understand the great mercies and favors that the Father of mercies and graces has bestowed upon you recently: that is, though you are poor and miserable captives, occupied day and night in great afflictions and bodily labors, and besides not being practiced in the reading of the Holy Scripture, rather being quite alienated from it, and therefore Christians only in name, His Majesty, moved not by your merits or by good deeds you might have done, but by His great mercy, clemency, and kindness according to His eternal counsel and decree, has chosen to bring you out of the ignorance in which you were raised, and has revealed to you Jesus Christ our Redeemer. Therefore, since the day I heard this, I have not ceased to pray for you and ask God that you may be filled with all knowledge of His will, in all wisdom and spiritual understanding, so that you may walk as is worthy of your reformed Christian religion that you profess, pleasing the

Lord in everything, bearing fruit in all good works, and growing in the knowledge of God; strengthened with all might according to the power of His glory, in all tolerance and patience and long-suffering, with joy, so that you may no longer be Christians only in name, as you were before, but in the reality of truth. And thus, as confirmation that you truly confess Christ, you have suffered for Him and had conflicts with the adversaries and enemies of the cross of Christ, who wanted to take away and strip you of such a great good and treasure as is that which Jesus Christ, our Redeemer, has now anew made for you, manifesting Himself to you and making Himself known much more clearly than before.

1.1 A *Dead* Faith and a *Living* Faith

Because your faith, which you had before, was only a historical faith, a dead faith, such as the wicked and even the demons themselves have, who, as James says in chapter 2, verse 19, believe and tremble. In addition to having such a faith that does not please God, your religion, which you thought was Christian, was founded not on the Word of God, but on dreams, illusions of the devil, and false miracles; such as those that confirm purgatory, those that affirm transubstantiation, making people believe that the bread and wine, which we eat and drink and which become part of our substance (but, administered according to the Lord's institution, are sacraments of the true body and blood of Christ) cease to be bread and wine and become the body and blood of Christ. And so they dream that if in a hundred thousand places at one moment and time a hundred thousand masses were said, in each of them would be the true body and blood of Christ, and the same Christ really and carnally, as large and as great as He was on the cross. This is contrary to what true Christians profess, that there is only one Jesus Christ and that this Jesus Christ has only one body, according to which He was born, lived in the world, died, rose again, ascended to heaven and is not here below in bodily presence, but is seated at the right hand of the Father, from where He will not descend until the last day, when He comes to judge the living and the dead as we confess in the creed. This confession is very different from that of our adversaries.

Besides this, they give so much authority to a man, a sinner, a man of sin and son of perdition whom they call the Pope, making him God on earth, in heaven, in hell, and in purgatory; and if there were more places, they would make him

God in all of them. They believe he cannot err, and being infallible, he is not subject to the judgment of any living person, nor even of the angels; and thus, he disregards princes, kings, emperors, councils, and the entire universal church. This man, like God, forgives sins, invents new articles of faith, and declares as heretics all those who do not believe them; he leads people to honor God with new forms of worship that God never commanded, such as invoking the saints. Those with eye ailments invoke Saint Lucia, those with toothaches Saint Apollonia, those with throat issues Saint Blas, etc., and they go even further; they are not content with invoking the saints but also their images, their statues, or more accurately, their idols. Thus, when they find themselves in life-threatening danger, when they see the ship they are on sinking, some will say, "*My Lady of Montserrat!*" others, "*Mother of God of Guadalupe!*" others, "*Saint Mary of the Old!*" Of God, of His son Jesus Christ, who is the only intercessor and mediator with the Father, hardly anyone remembers. We never read that the Blessed Virgin, Saint Peter, Saint Paul, any of the apostles, patriarchs, or prophets said, "Call upon me in the day of tribulation, and I will deliver you;" but we read in many passages of Scripture that God commands us to invoke Him in tribulation; and He gives His word, which will never fail, that He will deliver us. I am content with one passage from Psalm 50, verse 15: "Call upon me, says God, in the day of distress; I will deliver you, and you will honor me." Note that God says, when man invokes God, God receives this service as honor due to Him; and being a jealous God, He does not want His honor to be given to any creature. In this respect, the poor papists go on pilgrimages, some to this image, others to that, according to their foolish devotion; God will rightly say to them, "Who required these things at your hands?" To such people, it is just to say what God said to the Jewish people (Isaiah 29:13), which is the same as what the Lord said to the Scribes and Pharisees (Matthew 15:9): "In vain do they worship me, teaching as doctrines the commandments of men."

What shall I say here about the virtues they claim their holy water possesses? Every Sunday, the priest first exorcises (as they call it) the salt and then the water; having done this, he mixes the salt into the water and goes to the church to sprinkle it over the people. I remember well that the priest, while performing the *asperges*[1] (as they call this sprinkling), would say: "*aqua benedicta sit vobis salus et vita*," meaning, "*may the holy water be to you health and life*." A terrible blasphemy against the Divine Majesty. Isn't this taking glory from God and giving it to a creature? They believe that this holy water gives health to the body and benefits the soul, and that it is effective against evil spirits, and that it cleanses not only humans but even inanimate objects. Thus, they sprinkle it on the ground, on stones, on graves; and the priest prays to God to give it this strength and virtue. It is also used for women; because the first time they go out after childbirth, they go to the church, and the priest greets them at the door with his aspergillum[2] in hand and sprinkles them, and thus they are purified with this water. In conclusion, this water serves for many things; but mainly for conjuring spirits, especially at night, and the conjurer feels very safe from devils if he has holy water by his side, which then becomes

---

1. The Catholic rite of sprinkling a congregation with holy water prior to principle Mass on Sunday, from the Latin *aspergere*, which means "to wash" or "to sprinkle."

2. A Catholic liturgical instrument used for the asperges, the sprinkling of holy water.

his god. It is also used to bless and sanctify all the ornaments for saying Mass; they sprinkle it on the place where a church is to be built, and when it is built, the bishop sprinkles the top of the walls, then the middle, and then the lower parts. It would never end to speak of the virtues of holy water. In conclusion, holy water serves for the papists everything that lustral water served for the pagans.

Also, according to their traditions and dreams, bells have great virtues, especially against storms and evil spirits. But for the bells to have virtue, they must be baptized and anointed with chrism; thus, they are given the names of this or that saint. It's notable that, according to them, the baptism of bells is much more excellent than that of creatures, because any priest and any person, even women and midwives among them, can baptize creatures; but only the bishop can baptize bells. What is mocking and scorning holy baptism if this is not? The books of our adversaries are full of false miracles, phantoms, and spirits that were heard, and of souls of the deceased who spoke with this or that person: some indicated their miserable state in hell, others said they were suffering severe torments in purgatory; but they would be freed from those pains and thus go to heaven if certain masses were said for them, if certain things were done in their place, or certain vows they had promised but not fulfilled were completed. Most of these visions were inventions of the clergy, who, to fill their bellies, to have good food and better wine to drink, said that the soul of so-and-so had appeared to them and said this or that. The superstition of the people was so great that there were devout women who offered to tell you where the soul of your father, mother, husband, wife, or any other person you wished was, by doing certain things and saying certain devotions, such as the seven penitential psalms, the prayer of the enclosed, the count's prayer, the prayer of the just judge, or the prayer of Saint Brigid and other such superstitions; but it was necessary to give them so much wax and the crested hen and other things. Other apparitions were illusions of the devil to deceive the simple common folk, making them believe that the mass, pilgrimages, and other similar things were very holy and very good; and that as such, they greatly helped the souls in purgatory. All of this was just judgment and punishment from God, letting them be deceived by the devil, since they did not believe in the word of God written in the Holy Scripture.

I will recount a story, often mentioned by many. A certain priest took several beetles and attached small burning candles to them, then let them loose in the cemetery. These beetles, moving around among the graves at night, caused great alarm among the ignorant who saw them and were unaware of the cleric's trickery. Thus, the entire town, thinking these were souls from purgatory, was astonished and amazed. The next day, the cunning cleric ascended the pulpit and preached to them that these souls were coming to ask for assistance and help from the living, urging them to have a certain number of masses said, which, once performed, would release them from the pains they were enduring. However, the deception and mockery of religion by the cleric was discovered because some of the beetles, with their extinguished candles, were found among the rubbish in the cemetery, which the cleric had failed to collect.

Note what we said about false miracles in the *Treatise on the Mass*,[3] and in the following pages about the soul of Trajan and Falconilla, who, as they believe, came out of hell and went to heaven;

---

3. This may have been a reference to Valera's *Dos Tratados del Papa y de la Misa*, or to a work now lost to us, it is unclear but it is more likely the first.

the former through the prayers of the first martyr, and the latter through those of Saint Gregory; also, what we said about the skull that revealed to Macarius what was happening in purgatory. I cannot omit here to recount what happened in Seville about forty years ago or a little more. The priests of *omnium Sanctorum* (which is one of the parishes of Seville) one day, while conversing, lamented that few masses were being said. The sacristan, who overheard them and was also losing his share, told them that he knew a very good way to make people come for masses. When asked how, he said to leave it to him. He then gathered all the bones of the deceased that were in the cemetery and had someone preach about the diligence that had been put into collecting the bones for burial; and since they were to be buried, it would be very well done to say some masses for them; and who should order them and do so much good, if not the neighbors of that parish, who were relatives and friends of those deceased? The gravedigger knew how to paint the matter so well and persuade the people in such a way that masses poured in, and thus a solemn burial was held.

What we should believe about these phantoms and spirits, which they say appear, is that they are not the souls of the deceased, but either

illusions of the devil to further deceive the ignorant common folk, or inventions of the clergy
to extract money from the pockets of those who
think that everything the clergy tell them is true.
In the entire Holy Scripture, there is no testimony
or example that the souls of the dead appear to
the living; therefore, it should not be believed that
the spirit of Samuel appeared to Saul, but rather
that the witch, by the art of the devil, made some
demon appear in the form and figure of Samuel
to completely deceive Saul, already rejected by
God. Besides this, the express commandment
that forbids consulting such spirits clearly declares
these appearances to be mere illusions of the
devil. Deuteronomy 18:10-12 says, "Let no one
be found among you who practices divination or
sorcery, interprets omens, engages in witchcraft,
or casts spells, or who is a medium or spiritist or
who consults the dead. Anyone who does these
things is detestable to the Lord."

In the parable that the Lord tells in Luke 16, it
confirms what we are saying. When the rich man
begged Abraham to send Lazarus to his father's
house because, he says, I have five brothers so that
he may warn them, so they do not also come to
this place of torment, what does Abraham reply?
They have Moses and the prophets: let them listen

to them. The rich man responded: No, father Abraham; but if someone from the dead goes to them, they will repent. But Abraham said to him: If they do not listen to Moses and the prophets, they will not be convinced even if someone rises from the dead. The great Athanasius asks if it's possible to know why God does not allow the soul of any dead person to appear in this world. He answers himself, saying that this would be a cause of many errors and deceptions, because the devil would want no better opportunity to transform himself and take the form of this or that person, and saying that he came from the other world, he would tell many lies and deceive many. Chrysostom, on chapter 8 of Matthew, says that it is impossible for the soul of any dead person to return to this world or appear to anyone. He says the same in his second homily on Lazarus. As for the souls of Trajan and Falconilla, they are just dreams. By faith, we understand that there is no redemption in hell, and that once someone enters it by just and irrevocable judgment of God, they will never leave it. The reason is that in hell there is no repentance of sins with trust in the mercy of God through Christ. And where there is no such thing, there is no forgiveness of sins. As for their pretended miracles, we vividly remember the holy nun of Lisbon, who was condemned on December 6, 1588. She was another Magdalena de la Cruz. It is noteworthy that wherever the reformation of the Gospel has begun to be preached in our times, all these false miracles and illusions of the devil have ceased. The devil sees that they understand, and therefore he will gain nothing, and so he stops bothering in that way; but as cunning and old fox that he is, he invents others: such is the hatred he has for mankind.

Enough has been said about the traditions, apparitions, and delusions concocted by our adversaries who think they are serving God in this way. True Christian religion does not concern itself with such follies. It knows that in the worship and manner of honoring God, the only thing that pleases God is what He has commanded through His own words, as recorded by His holy prophets and apostles in the book we call the Holy Scripture. Thus, God often says when speaking to His people: do what I command you; and the prophets, to confirm and seal what they have said, conclude by saying: God has spoken. It knows that there is no other remission of sins but through the blood of Christ alone, which we partake in by faith. It knows that the sacrament of baptism should not be profaned, and that Christ did not command the baptism of bells or ships (which they also baptize), but only of creatures, children of faithful parents, who are children of the promise God made to Abraham, saying: "I will be your God and the God of your descendants after you." It knows that only God should be invoked, not with superstitions, false miracles, feigned apparitions, illusions of the devil, or idolatries, but in spirit and truth: and not in this place or that place, but everywhere. For God is no longer the God of just one nation, but of the whole world, and of all His church, which is called catholic or universal, because it is not confined to one place but is spread throughout the world. And as the children of this age are more prudent than the children of light in their way, the antichrist has found a marvelous means to maintain his kingdom and keep his followers in their ignorance, superstitions, and idolatries. He entertains them with dreams, feigned apparitions, false miracles, and the authority of the pope, whom they believe (but without any word from God) cannot err.

1.2 An Exhortation to Read the Scriptures

Regarding the Pope, the popes for many years now have been greedy, ambitious, rebellious, lustful, and corrupt in life and doctrine; they are men of sin and sons of perdition; *antichrists*, to sum it up in one word, as has been sufficiently proven in the book about the authority of the pope that God used as an instrument for you to recognize the abuses and superstitions of the papacy, so that you might truly be Christians. And to prevent their false doctrine from being recognized as false, the Pope forbids the people from hearing, seeing, or even imagining reading or contemplating the Holy Scripture, which is the only means that God, in His great mercy, has left in the world to know, understand, and recognize what is the true religion and what is false, what is the worship and manner of honoring Him that He commands and with which He is pleased, and what is that which He forbids and detests. This is the sole cause of all the heresies, errors, ignorance, superstitions, and idolatries that exist in the papacy, the ignorance, the not reading, the not meditating on Scripture. That's why the Lord says (Matt. 22:29): "You err because you do not know the Scriptures," and as St. John says in 5:39 of his Gospel: "Search the Scriptures," said Christ, etc., and then says: "They are the ones that testify about me." As if to say: You want to know God and His Christ? Read the Scriptures, because he who does not read them will

23

neither know the Father nor the Son. When a certain person asked the Lord how he would possess eternal life, Christ sent him to what the law said: "What is written in the law? How do you read it?" David, in Psalm 1, speaking of the pious man, says that his delight is in the law of the Lord, and in His law, he will meditate day and night.

But setting aside the many places where God commands everyone in general and each person in particular to read the Scripture, that great and admirable Psalm 119, which papist clerics sing or recite every day, and which so few of them understand, contains praises for the law of God and His word. It vehemently and emphatically encourages the Christian, the pious, those who desire and strive to serve God, to read and meditate on the word of God. The reading and meditation of God's word, accompanied by invoking the Spirit of the Lord to enlighten our understanding so that we may comprehend and benefit from the Scripture, is necessary for all, whether young or old, rich or poor, educated or uneducated. And so it says, "Your word is a lamp for my feet, a light on my path." And at the beginning, David had asked how a young man could cleanse his way, meaning, how a youth could live in purity; he answers,

"By guarding your word." I ask them now: how will either the old or the young guard the word of God, or how will it be a light on their paths, when they neither know nor understand what it is? When they do not read or meditate on it, nor call upon the Lord to enlighten their understanding to comprehend it? And if this dispute over reading Scripture were to be settled by what the ancient doctors and councils say (not the modern ones, where the antichrist of Rome has presided), we could easily confirm what we say, for there is not one of them who does not exhort to read and hear the Holy Scripture.

Among them all, St. John Chrysostom remarkably exhorts in many places every kind of person, men and women, young and old, rich and poor, etc., to read the Scriptures. He himself responds to all the objections that our adversaries today raise against the reading of the Scripture. But among all his works, the third sermon he made on Lazarus is particularly admirable. At the beginning of this sermon, he says: It is my custom to tell you many days in advance the subject I am going to discuss so that in the meantime you may take your book and, noting the entirety of what can be discussed, after having understood what has been said, you may prepare to hear what remains. And this I always exhort and will never cease to exhort, that you not only pay attention here (he means in the church) to what is said to you, but also, when you are at home, you continually practice the reading of the Holy Scripture. He then responds to the objections, saying: Let no one tell me, I have enough to understand in the affairs of the state, I am a magistrate; I am an artisan living off the work of my hands, I am married, have a wife, children, and a family to provide for; I am a man of the world, and therefore it is not fitting for me to read the Scripture, but for those who have left the world and gone to the wilderness. To which he replies: What are you saying, oh man? It is not fitting for you to delve into the Scriptures because you are distracted with many cares? On the contrary, I tell you that it is more your duty than that of the others, etc. And he gives the reason, saying, those who have withdrawn from the world do not have as much need to read the Scripture as those who are, so to speak, in the midst of the sea, tossed here and there by the waves. Such people, he says, always need the continuous comfort of the Scripture. Those who are withdrawn are sitting far from the battle and therefore do not receive many wounds.

But you, because you are continuously in battle, because you are often wounded, therefore you have more need for remedies like one who is provoked by their spouse, saddened and angered by their child, stalked by an enemy, or envied by a friend. Chrysostom continues this discourse and concludes by saying: therefore, it is necessary to ceaselessly take up arms from the Scripture. And a little further down: it is now impossible, I say, for anyone to be saved if they do not continually engage in spiritual reading, etc. And then: Do you not see that blacksmiths, silver-smiths, and all those engaged in any mechanical art have all their tools and all the instruments of their art ready and in order? Even if they are very poor and hunger plagues them, still they would rather suffer hunger than sell any of their tools for food, etc. Likewise: certainly, we should have the same mindset as them. And just as the tools of their art are the hammer, the anvil, the tongs, similarly our tools are the books of the apostles and prophets and all Scripture divinely inspired and useful, etc. Also, let us not be negligent in acquiring these books to avoid being struck by a mortal wound. Additionally, the mere sight of the books causes us not to be so quick to sin. If we have committed something forbidden, upon returning home and looking at the books, our conscience condemns us more vehemently, etc. Another objection he addresses is one that some in our times make. What will it be, they say, if we do not understand what is contained in the books? Chrysostom responds: Even if you do not understand the mysteries of Scripture, still, the mere reading of Scripture brings about a certain holiness in us; although it cannot be that you are ignorant of everything you read.

For the grace of the Spirit has thus dispensed and tailored everything in the Scripture so that tax collectors, fishermen, artisans, shepherds, apostles, the uneducated, and the uninformed could be saved through these books. This ensures that no one can use ignorance as an excuse, claiming the Scripture is obscure; so that what is said in it can be easily understood by all. This way, the artisan, the servant, the widow, and even the most ignorant of all people can gain some benefit and profit from having heard the Scripture read, etc. Additionally, the apostles and prophets clearly and plainly set forth their teachings to all as common instructors of the world, so that each person could learn from the reading alone. And this, foretold by the prophet, said: all will be taught by God, and no one will say to their neighbor, 'Know the

Lord,' for they will all know me, from the least to the greatest, etc. This was said by Isaiah in chapter 54, verse 13, Jeremiah in 31, verse 34, and John in 6, verse 45. Chrysostom also says: Besides this, aren't the signs, miracles, and stories manifest and clear things that everyone understands?

So, it is merely an excuse and a cover for laziness to say that what is in the Scripture is not understandable. How can you ever understand something that you don't even care to glance at occasionally? Take the book in your hands, read the whole story, and retain in your memory what is clear; and what is obscure and not very clear, read it many times; and if with continual reading you still cannot understand it, go to someone wise, to some learned person, and discuss with them what you have read, etc. Additionally, reading Scripture is a powerful weapon against sin; ignorance of Scripture is a great abyss and a profound ocean; it is a great loss for salvation not to know anything about the divine laws: ignorance of the scriptures is the cause of heresies; this ignorance leads people to live poorly, it upsets everything from top to bottom because it cannot be, I say it cannot be, that someone who reads Scripture continuously and attentively remains unbenefited, etc. All this and much more is said by Saint Chrysostom in the mentioned sermon, which I have summarized as much as possible.

From this, we can clearly see how impiously the Pope has forbidden the Christian people from reading the word of God, which goes against the express commandment of God and against what the prophets, Christ, His apostles, and ancient teachers taught. This teaching is what the holy martyrs of Jesus Christ suffered martyrdom for. It is an explicit commandment from God in Deuteronomy 17:18, where He instructs the king to have the law of God written in a book, to keep this book, and to read from it all the days of his life. The purpose of reading this Scripture is then stated: so that he may learn to fear the Lord his God, to keep all the words of this law and these statutes to do them, etc.

And so, in accordance with this decree, the good Emperor Theodosius II, a descendant of Spanish lineage, himself wrote the entire New Testament by his own hand and had a custom of reading it every morning. The empress, his wife, named Eudoxia, a woman well-versed in Scripture, and the emperor's sisters were present at these readings. About Alfred, King of England, it is said that he divided the twenty-four hours of the day and night into three parts: eight hours were spent reading, praying, and meditating; another eight in the administration of his kingdom, and the remaining eight fulfilling the needs of his body. Of Emperor Charlemagne, it is read that he was very devoted to reading the Holy Scripture. The King of Spain, Receswinth or Rocsinth, who died in the year 672, among other virtues attributed to him, had an insatiable thirst to know the secret mysteries of the Holy Scripture and thus never was without the company of great theologians, to whom he would regularly ask profound and necessary questions for his salvation. This is mentioned by Doctor Illescas in his pontifical on John VII.

The same author, speaking of Gregory V, says that Robert, King of France, among other virtues, was wonderfully learned in both sacred and secular letters. The same author mentions that Don Alonso I, known as the Catholic, diligently collected the books of the Holy Scripture that were in the possession of the infidels. Our good King Recaredo, being so well-versed in the reading of Scripture, himself with his wise reasoning convinced many Arian priests, and thus more with reason than with the authority of a king, he converted them to true Christian religion. If only the kings of today would imitate these holy kings by reading the Holy Scripture, meditating on it, and praying; and not heed what the Pope forbids them, which is not to read the Scripture, but rather heed what God commands them to read. Let the Pope then consider the account he will have to give to God for having deceived the world. Therefore, it should not be surprising if for this and other similar reasons we call him the antichrist, for he is.

In discussing this abuse, I have been somewhat lengthy, but it will be forgiven, given the necessity for my fellow Spaniards to know and understand this. May the Lord grant them grace to benefit from what their compatriot, desiring to advise them on the most crucial aspect of their salvation, has told them. At least consider whether I speak the truth, whether the Scripture says what I have told you, whether the fathers, and especially St. John Chrysostom in the cited place, say what has been attributed to them. Therefore, my brothers, you owe infinite thanks to God who, in your bodily captivity, has given you the true freedom of the spirit. You had a confused, dead, and historical faith, not knowing what you believed: now God has given you, through hearing His word, a clear and living faith: you believe with certain confidence in divine mercy, that through the blood of Jesus Christ, and not by any other means (for there is none), you are justified before the gaze of the Father, and as such, you must perform good works and flee from evil ones. Be grateful, then. May His Majesty continue the good work He has begun in you. It is not enough to start well; it is necessary to persevere. And he who perseveres to the end will be saved. Do not promise yourselves great riches in this world for being truly Christian; our riches are in heaven, where you will have no misery, no hunger or affliction, no captivity, no slaps or shoves, no beatings or whippings; all this will have passed, and blessed is he who has suffered it patiently for the Lord's name; his reward will be very great. May the Lord grant you the grace to be steadfast in the confession of His name. Read the Holy Scripture, and if you cannot read, listen when others read or discuss it; meditate and ruminate on what you have read or heard; invoke the Lord to teach you with His Spirit, for all our efforts are in vain if His Majesty does not bless them.

What remains is to comfort you and give you some guidance on how to conduct yourselves in the undertaking you have embraced. There are many places in Scripture that serve this purpose, but the first epistle of Saint Peter seemed particularly apt for this. Therefore, I advise you to read it; and if you do not have the book, I will make here a summary of the main points contained in it that are relevant to your situation. Saint Peter wrote this epistle to the faithful who had converted from Judaism to Christ, and who were exiled from their land that God had given them and were scattered across various parts of the world. As Saint Peter was the apostle to the Jews just as Saint Paul was to the Gentiles, he writes this letter to console them in their afflictions, in their needs, in their hunger and nakedness, in their exile and captivity. He exhorts them to have patience, as this is the royal road by which God leads His children and by which He led Christ, of whom he says was afflicted for us, leaving us an example so that you may follow in his footsteps. He confirms them in the faith in Christ which they had received, etc.

The epistle begins by addressing not only the converted Jews of that time but also you, Christians converted to true Christianity. It says: Peter, an apostle of Jesus Christ, to the foreigners scattered in Pontus, etc.; *to the foreigners who are captives in the land of the Moors*, chosen according to the foreknowledge of God the Father, in sanctification of the Spirit, for obedience and sprinkling with the blood of Jesus Christ; *this is the true asperges, not that of the water they call holy*; may grace and peace be multiplied to you. Blessed be the God and Father of our Lord Jesus Christ, who according to His great mercy has regenerated us into a living hope through the resurrection of Jesus Christ from the dead, for an inheritance incorruptible, undefiled, and that fades not away, reserved in heaven for you who are kept by the power of God through faith for salvation ready to be revealed in the last time. In this you greatly rejoice, though now for a little while; if need be, you are grieved by various trials, so that the genuineness of your faith, much more precious than gold that perishes, though it is tested by fire, may be found to praise, honor, and glory at the revelation of Jesus Christ, whom having not seen you yet love; in whom, though now you see Him not, yet believing, you rejoice with joy unspeakable and full of glory, receiving the end of your faith— the salvation of your souls, etc.

Furthermore: therefore, gird up the loins of your mind, be sober, and rest your hope fully upon the grace that is to be brought to you at the revelation of Jesus Christ; as obedient children, not conforming yourselves to the former lusts, as in your ignorance under *Papism*. But as

He who called you is holy, you also be holy in all your conduct, etc. You were redeemed from your aimless conduct received by tradition from your fathers, not with corruptible things like silver or gold, but with the precious blood of Christ, etc. Having purified your souls in obeying the truth through the Spirit in sincere brotherly love, love one another fervently with a pure heart, having been born again, not of corruptible seed but incorruptible, through the word of God which lives and abides forever. *This word was withheld from you by the Pope, and thus you could not be reborn in Christ*, of which this word (despite the Antichrist) endures forever; and this is the word which by the Gospel is now announced *to you in your exile and captivity*, etc.

Additionally: you, as living stones, are being built up a spiritual house, a holy priesthood, to offer up spiritual sacrifices acceptable to Jesus Christ, etc. So that you may proclaim the virtues of Him who has called you out of darkness (*in which you were all the time of your ignorance, before you were called to the true knowledge of Christ*) into His marvelous light (which is the true knowledge of Christ, and how we should serve the Father, not according to the commandments and traditions of men, but according to what His Majesty has commanded in His Holy Scripture, which you do well to read and listen to.) You, who in times past were not a people, but are now the people of God, who had not obtained mercy, but now have obtained mercy.

Beloved, I urge you as foreigners and sojourners, abstain from fleshly lusts which war against the soul, and have your conduct honorable among the Gentiles, *among Moors, Jews, and false Christians, in the midst of whom you dwell*, so that in what they speak against you as evildoers and heretics, *for having truly known Christ*, they may, by observing your good works, glorify God in the day of visitation. Therefore, submit yourselves to every ordinance of man for the Lord's sake, whether to the king as supreme, or to governors, as to those who are sent by Him for the punishment of evildoers and the praise of those who do good. For this is the will of God, that by doing good you may put to silence the ignorance of foolish men, etc. Servants, *you captives in the land of the Moors*, be submissive with all fear to your masters, not only to the good and gentle but also to the harsh. For this is commendable if, because of conscience toward God, one endures grief, suffering wrongfully. What glory is there if, when you sin, you are *slapped, beaten, whipped, and thrown into dungeons where you suffer great hunger and misery*, and endure it? But if you do well and *confess Jesus Christ, your Redeemer*, and are then afflicted and suffer for it, this is certainly pleasing to God. For this is what you are called to, *since Christ suffered for us. It is not a great thing that we should also suffer for Him*, for Christ suffered, leaving us an example that you, *poor captives*, should follow in His footsteps. *Suffer as He did*, He who committed no sin. *Who can say in truth that they have no sin?* In whose mouth no deceit was found. When He was cursed, He did not curse in return; when He suffered, He did not threaten, but entrusted Himself to Him who judges justly, etc. Also, by His wounds, you have been healed, for *before you truly knew Christ*, you were like sheep going astray, but now you have returned to the Shepherd and Overseer of your souls, etc.

Additionally: Be of one mind, having compassion for one another; love as brothers, be tenderhearted, be courteous; not returning evil for evil or reviling for reviling, but on the contrary blessing, knowing that you were called to this, that you may inherit a blessing. For "He who would love life and see good days, let him refrain his tongue from evil, and his lips from speaking deceit. Let him turn away from evil and do good;

let him seek peace and pursue it. For the eyes of the Lord are on the righteous, and His ears are *open* to their prayers. But the face of the Lord is against those who do evil." And who is he who will harm you if you become followers of what is good? But even if you should suffer for righteousness' sake, you are blessed. "And do not be afraid of their threats, nor be troubled." But sanctify the Lord God in your hearts, and always be ready to give a defense to everyone who asks you a reason for the hope that is in you (*and for the reason why you have left the Pope*), with meekness and fear; having a good conscience, that when they defame you as evildoers, those who revile your good conduct in Christ may be ashamed. For it is better, if it is the will of God, to suffer for doing good than for doing evil. For Christ also suffered once for sins, the just for the unjust, that He might bring us to God, being put to death in the flesh but made alive by the Spirit, etc.

Furthermore: Since Christ suffered for us in the flesh, arm yourselves also with the same mind, for he who has suffered in the flesh has ceased from sin, so that he no longer should live the rest of his time in the flesh for the lusts of men, but for the will of God. For we have spent enough of our past lifetime in doing the will of the Gentiles—*or the anti-Christians of our time*—when we walked in *gluttony, drunkenness, ignorance, superstitions, blasphemies*, and abominable idolatries (such as those you committed, thinking to render great service to the Blessed Virgin, making her equal with God, who alone is Almighty, who chose and created her to be the mother, according to the flesh, of our Redeemer Jesus Christ).

The hymn that begins with "*Ave maris stella*" is filled with similar blasphemies, such as when it says: "Establish us in peace, moving the name of Eve, release the guilty from their chains, give light to the blind, relieve our evils, ask for all good things. Show yourself to be a mother," meaning: *Understand, my child, whom you have; you are his mother*. And a little further down: "Make us, free from guilt, affable and chaste. Grant a pure life, make the path safe." Also, in the hymn that begins with "*quem terra, pontus* etc.," at the end, there are these words: "Mary, mother of grace, mother of mercy, defend us from the enemy, and receive us at the hour of death." The prayer that begins with "*Salve regina, mater misericordiae* etc." is filled with similar blasphemies. Listen to the reason why I say this: because the honor and glory that belong to the eternal God and to His Son Christ, such as forgiving sins, being the father of grace and mercy, making the blind see, etc., His Majesty does not share with any creature, no matter how holy, as seen by what God Himself says speaking with the Messiah, our Christ, in Isaiah 42:6-8 (which proves the Messiah to be true God, as He does what only the LORD does): "I, the Lord, have called You in righteousness, and will hold Your hand; I will keep You and give You as a covenant to the people, as a light to the Gentiles, to open blind eyes, to bring out prisoners from the prison, those who sit in darkness from the prison house; I am the Lord, that is My name; and My glory I will not give to another, nor My praise to carved images."

The Blessed Virgin, while she lived in this world, would have been very careful not to accept such flattery and foolish devotions; for they were blasphemies against the majesty of the Heavenly Father, who created her, of Christ, who redeemed her, and of the Holy Spirit who sanctified her and adorned her with as many virtues as were fitting for her who was to be the mother of our Redeemer Jesus Christ, true God and true man. Therefore, she would not want to hear them now either. Those who think they are rendering her great service with such acts are not serving her at all, but rather causing her great displeasure and dishonor.

41

The true honor with which we should honor the Blessed Virgin and the other saints is to follow their footsteps, to be their imitators, as they were of Christ. And so Saint Paul says, speaking to the Corinthians in his first letter, chapter 11, verse 1: "Imitate me, just as I also imitate Christ." (*But let's return to our Apostle Saint Peter.*)

It seems strange to those who malign you that you do not run with them into the same excess of dissipation. They will have to give an account to Him who is ready to judge the living and the dead, etc. Furthermore, the end of all things is near. Therefore, be sober-minded and watchful in prayer. And above all, have fervent love among yourselves, for love will cover a multitude of sins. (These last words Saint Peter took from Proverbs 10:12, where it is clear what he means by them.) Solomon says: "Hatred stirs up strife, but love covers all sins." As if to say: a person who harbors hatred towards another reveals all the evil they know about them, and thus they bite and consume each other in vengeance; but on the contrary, one who has love, who loves, covers, overlooks, and pretends not to see the faults; and even if offended seventy times seven times, forgives, in accordance with what the Lord commands in Matthew 18:22. Therefore, our adversaries very wrongly use this passage to imply that almsgiving and other acts of charity are recompense before God for the forgiveness of sins.

(Saint Peter continues): If anyone speaks, let him speak as the oracles of God, etc. Beloved, do not think it strange concerning the fiery trial which is to try you, as though some strange thing happened to you; but rejoice to the extent that you partake of Christ's sufferings, that when His glory is revealed, you may also be glad with exceeding joy. If you are reproached for the name of Christ, blessed are you, for the Spirit of glory and of God rests upon you. On their part, He is blasphemed, but on your part, He is glorified. Therefore, let none of you suffer as a murderer, a thief, an evildoer, or as a busybody in other people's matters. Yet if anyone suffers as a Christian, let him not be ashamed, but let him glorify God in this matter. For the time has come for judgment to begin at the house of God; and if it begins with us first, what will be the end of those who do not obey the gospel of God? And if the righteous one is scarcely saved, where will the ungodly and the sinner appear? Therefore, let those who suffer according to the will of God commit their souls to Him in doing good, as to a faithful Creator, etc.

Furthermore: humble yourselves under the mighty hand of God, that He may exalt you in due time; casting all your care upon Him, for He cares for you. Be sober, be vigilant; because your adversary the devil walks about like a roaring lion, seeking whom he may devour. Resist him, steadfast in the faith, knowing that the same sufferings are experienced by your brotherhood in the world. But may the God of all grace, who has called us to His eternal glory by Christ Jesus, after you have suffered a while, perfect, establish, strengthen, and settle you, etc. *Saint Peter thus concludes his epistle, so necessary for the poor, foreign, and afflicted Christians of that time, and equally necessary now for you poor Christians, foreigners, afflicted and captives in Barbary, saying:* Peace to you all who are in Christ Jesus, Amen. *This means, those who believe in their heart and confess with their mouth that Jesus Christ is their Redeemer, and that there is no other means by which your sins can be forgiven except through His intercession, death, and passion.*

1.3 Persecution is to be Expected

I want to warn you about something so that you are not scandalized or offended when you see or hear it wherever the Gospel is preached (which is the good news given to us, that the eternal

Father graciously, without any self-interest, but solely through Christ, forgives our sins), and especially when it is first preached, there arise tumults and disturbances; father is set against son and son against father; some believe, others blaspheme and become even worse than before. This has always been the case, is the case, and always will be. When God begins to build His Church, Satan immediately builds his chapel within it, which often becomes so large that the Church of God is overshadowed. When God initially planted His Church in the righteous Abel, Satan immediately built his in the wicked Cain, who persecuted Abel for being good, just, and holy, and did not stop until he killed him. Those in Noah's time mocked what Noah preached to them. The same happened with the people of Sodom towards Lot. The Philistines pursued Abraham, Isaac, and Jacob, who were the Church of God. Ishmael mocked Isaac, Esau persecuted his brother Jacob, and Saul pursued David.

And moving to the New Testament, when Christ preached His Gospel in Jerusalem and other parts of Judea, what upheavals there were! Some said: He speaks well, He preaches well, He is a prophet, He is the Messiah; others said: He is a deceiver, a blasphemer, a troublemaker, a

Samaritan (meaning: a heretic), He is possessed, He performs miracles by the power of Beelzebub. Jerusalem was in turmoil; the Scribes, Pharisees, Doctors of the Law, the Priests, and especially the High Priests could not tolerate His doctrine and were His greatest enemies. Driven by their furious hatred (because Christ exposed their deceptions and hypocrisies and clarified the true worship with which God wishes to be honored), they did not stop until they had Him killed, and in the most shameful way then known: death on a cross. This form of death was used to remove from the world those considered unworthy to live in it, the worst scoundrels, abominable and desperate people. At that time, crucifixion served the same purpose as burning at the stake does now. On the day of Pentecost, when the Holy Spirit visibly descended upon the apostles and they began to publicly preach the Gospel of the crucified Christ, what upheavals there were in Jerusalem! Some were amazed, others said: they are drunk. Even while the apostles were in Jerusalem, there arose the contentious question that has caused so much harm and continues to do so in the church of God: whether faith in Christ is sufficient for salvation or whether the works commanded by the law are necessary. This question was settled in the first Christian council held in Jerusalem, as we will see later. When the apostles left Jerusalem and went to preach the Gospel throughout the world, as Christ had commanded them, how were they received? The world could not tolerate their doctrine, it persecuted and killed the apostles and others who professed the law of Christ. This hatred was the cause of so many martyrs in the church of God, so many who died for the doctrine of the Gospel, for the faith in Jesus Christ.

This same hatred is held by the Scribes and Pharisees of our times, meaning the clerics and friars, the wise men of the world, the bishops, cardinals, and especially the popes, against the Reformation. Both in terms of doctrine and customs, learned and pious men sent by God to gather the remnants of Israel, meaning the faithful, motivated solely by the glory of God and the salvation of souls, and putting their honor and life in great peril, have preached, and by the mercy of God, still preach today for the great service of God and the salvation of souls. And all the cunning, strategies, and inventions of our adversaries, all their persecutions, confiscations of property, defamations, imprisonments, whippings, exiles, forced labor in galleys, killings, and burnings have not been able nor succeeded in extinguishing this fire, this evangelical doctrine that the Holy Spirit has ignited and wishes to burn, spread, and flourish throughout the world before the second coming of the Lord. As we see, it has spread throughout Christendom and even within Spain, which is the nation most opposed to this reformation, it has entered not insignificantly but among nobles, distinguished and illustrious people, learned and pious individuals. I refer to the numerous trials and inquisitions conducted in Spain in this regard.

It is noteworthy, a demonstration of God's power, that the more our adversaries persecute and burn, the more the number of the faithful grows; for the blood of the martyrs is the seed (as Tertullian aptly said) of the Gospel. The faithful are like the grain of wheat, which, to bear fruit, to yield thirtyfold, sixtyfold, or a hundredfold, must first die. These preachers of reformation, imitating Christ, the prophets, and apostles, condemn the ostentation, pride, greed, and ambition of the ecclesiastics, their bad lives and worse doctrine. They want and strive for all this to be reformed according to what God commands in Holy Scripture, which the prophets, Christ, and His apostles preached, and which the early Church observed; because the first (as Saint Cyprian says) is the true. And that shall prevail.

When Saint Paul sought to correct the abuses that had entered the Church of Corinth regarding the Holy Sacrament of the Lord's Supper, the best remedy he found was to bring the Supper celebrated by the Corinthians back to its original institution, so that they would neither add to nor take away from it, but celebrate it just as Jesus Christ, its institutor, had celebrated it. Thus, he says in 1 Corinthians 11:23, "For I received from the Lord that which I also delivered to you, etc." This is exactly what those currently seeking reformation are doing. They aim to remove the abuses that have been introduced in the celebration of baptism and the Lord's Supper, in the doctrine of justification and invocation, and in other matters, and to have these sacraments celebrated as Christ celebrated them. In a word, they desire that everything be regulated by the word of God. In matters of religion, where the salvation of souls is at stake, they do not want to be guided by dreams, inventions, or traditions of men, but by Holy Scripture.

See here, my brothers, the reason why, when the word of God is first preached, the world cannot bear it and, unable to bear it, arms itself against it. But the Christian will not want to have peace with the world by doing what the world does, which is to persecute Christ, His doctrine, and those who follow it; rather, he will wage war against it, even if he is a person of no account in the eyes of the world, trusting in Him who said, "In the world you will have tribulation; but be of good cheer, I have overcome the world." The Lord warned His disciples of this warfare in Matthew 10:34-35: "Do not think that I came to bring peace on earth. I did not come to bring peace, but a sword. For I have come to set a man against his father, a daughter against her mother," etc. The holy Simeon, when he took the child Jesus in his arms, said (as Luke recounts in chapter 2, verse 34 of his Gospel) to His mother Mary: "Behold, this Child is set for the fall and rising of many in Israel, and for a sign which will be spoken against." Isaiah, in chapter 8, verse 14, speaking of Christ, says the same. Saint Paul, quoting Isaiah in Romans 9:33, says: "Behold, I lay in Zion a stumbling stone and rock of offense, and whoever believes on Him will not be put to shame." Saint Peter also speaks of this stone in 1 Peter 2:6. This stone is Christ, upon whom Peter and all the other apostles and the entire Catholic Church, and each member of it in particular, are founded. Do not be offended, my brothers, or let it be a reason to turn back, the dissensions you hear and see because of the Gospel. The Lord has warned us about this. Know that this is one of the very certain marks and signs that the Gospel brings with it; when it is preached and announced, it divides the light from the darkness, shows what is the true doctrine and what is false, shows what is the worship and service that God commands and what He forbids, what are the works that please Him and what displeases Him.

May the Lord grant you grace so that, having overcome this temptation, which is great among beginners and causes some to turn back, you may go forward in confessing His name and say as Saint Peter did on behalf of the whole church, when the Lord asked His twelve apostles if they too wanted to turn back, if they wanted to leave Him, as some of the disciples had done: "Lord, to whom shall we go? You have the words of eternal life. And we believe and are sure that You are the Christ, the Son of the living God", John 6:68-69. This war that comes with the Gospel, properly speaking, is not caused by the Gospel, for it is a Gospel of peace, as Saint Paul calls it, and God, to whom the Gospel belongs, is an author of peace, His thoughts are of peace, not of dissension or war. The malice and hatred that worldly men without the Spirit of God have for the Gospel and for pure and sound doctrine are the cause of this war. If men, hearing sound doctrine, believed it, there would be no war, but great peace and tranquility. May God grant us the grace to obey the Gospel so that we may have peace; not the peace the world gives, but the peace that Christ so commended to His disciples. This peace is obtained only by those who are justified by faith. There is no one in the world as peaceful as the true Christian, regenerated by the Spirit of God. Such a person, when it comes to personal matters and not the glory of God, is very patient, endures and tolerates much for the sake of not breaking the peace.

Therefore, as you profess to be reformed Christians, you will necessarily have to face conflicts with three types of people while living in this land of Barbary: with anti-Christians, with Jews, and with Moors, and particularly with the devil, who will tempt you with various kinds of temptations. It is essential, then, to arm yourselves and be prepared against their assaults. The weapons are not carnal or earthly but spiritual, as Saint Paul describes (being a good warrior himself, always armed with them and having thoroughly tested and proven them). Speaking to the Ephesians, he says: "Put on the whole armor of God, that you may be able to stand against the wiles of the devil." Among other pieces with which the apostle arms the Christian, he names two very important ones: one is the shield, which he says is faith, with which you can quench all the fiery darts of the wicked one; the other is the sword, which he says is the word of God. As the apostle says (Hebrews 4:12), it is living and powerful, sharper than any two-edged sword, piercing even to the division of soul and spirit, and of joints and marrow, and is a discerner of the thoughts and intents of the heart. We would consider a soldier very foolish and insane who entered battle and wanted to fight against powerful and desperate mortal enemies without carrying weapons to defend himself or to attack the enemy.

Indeed, a Christian, whose life is a continual spiritual battle, is like that soldier if he does not arm himself with spiritual weapons of faith and the word of God. For faith to be alive and effective, it must be founded on the word of God. The word of God, to be efficacious and to work towards salvation, must be believed. From this, we see the great harm the Antichrist has done in the church of God by disarming the people of the principal piece of their armor, which is the word of God, which he forbids them to read under severe sanctions and penalties. How will they fight the enemy without a sword? After arming the Christian with all his weapons, the apostle commands continuous prayer, urging them to invoke God for assistance so that their enemies do not prevail against them, but are defeated and destroyed. The prayer of a righteous person (as James says in chapter 5, verse 16) is powerful and effective, which he confirms with the example of Elijah.

1.4 On Christian Life and Practice

The reading of Scripture and prayer are two very important practices for a Christian. When we pray, we speak with God, and when we read the word of God, God speaks with us. Let us listen to Him, then, if we want Him to hear us. In this battle I speak of, let no one presume on their own strength: let them humble themselves before the divine Majesty, asking that, through Christ, their faith may be increased and His word made clear to them. Such a person will be able to maintain their Christian religion through the word of God and confound the adversaries who speak against it. May His Majesty grant you the grace to persevere and grow in Him.

The name of Christian, when accompanied by the essential qualities that make one truly Christian, is very precious and highly esteemed in the sight of God. For the true and sincere Christian, one who follows in the footsteps of Christ, is a true reflection, a living portrait, and an exact image of Christ, and Christ is the image of the Father. God, who is invisible, has become visible and tangible in Christ. Everything that Christ is by nature, the Christian becomes through grace and adoption.

Thus, the Christian becomes a child of God, reborn as Saint Peter says, not of corruptible seed but of incorruptible, by the word of the living God (1 Peter 1:23). Saint John states that Christ gave the power to become children of God to all who received Him, to those who believe in His name (John 1:12). In this way, the Christian partakes in the divine nature. And just as Christ is a king, not of this world, having overcome sin, death, and the devil, so too is the Christian, who, with the strength given by his King, Christ, conquers these same enemies: sin, death, and the devil. As Christ is a priest, who offered Himself to the eternal Father, so the Christian offers himself, denying his own will and subjecting it to the law of God. Thus, through his High Priest Christ, he offers to

God a perpetual sacrifice, that is, as the apostle in Hebrews 13:15 describes: "the fruit of lips that openly profess His name."

And just as Christ is a prophet, who declares and teaches the will of His Father, so the Christian, being taught by God, speaks the word of God and things that edify; in accordance with what Saint Peter said: "If anyone speaks, let him speak as the oracles of God" (1 Peter 4:11). Unclean, vain, sharp, murmuring, and especially blasphemous words should be far from the mouth of a Christian. Great perfection is demanded of the Christian; but what is impossible for man is possible and very achievable for God, as the angel said to the Blessed Virgin when she asked how she could conceive without knowing a man: "For with God nothing will be impossible" (Luke 1:37). Hence, He is called Almighty. And the Christian, in a certain way, is too, which is why Saint Paul says in Philippians 4:13: "I can do all things through Christ who strengthens me."

What we have said about Christ being a king, priest, and prophet, and that, by the same token, every Christian, if truly Christian, is also a king, priest, and prophet, was well understood by Saint Peter. He reflected this understanding when speaking to all Christians and to each one of them, saying: "You are a chosen generation, a royal priesthood, a holy nation, etc." (1 Peter 2:9). This manner of speaking was adopted by Saint Peter from what God says in Exodus 19:5-6, speaking not only to the priests but to the entire house of Jacob, to all the people of Israel. "If you will indeed obey My voice and keep My covenant, then you shall be a special treasure to Me above all people; for all the earth is Mine. And you shall be to Me a kingdom of priests and a holy nation."

Saint John in the book of Revelation 1:6 also says: "He [Christ] has made us kings and priests to His God and Father," signifying a spiritual, not worldly, kingship and priesthood. Given the dignity, authority, and majesty of the Christian, it is only reasonable that they should not be cowardly, should not be brought low or trodden underfoot by the devil, should not become slaves to sin, and should not live according to the flesh. The works of the flesh, as listed by Saint Paul in Galatians 5:19-21, include adultery, fornication, uncleanness, lewdness, idolatry, sorcery, hatred, contentions, jealousies, outbursts of wrath, selfish ambitions, dissensions, heresies, envy, murders, drunkenness, revelries, and the like. Saint Paul warns that those who practice such things will not inherit the kingdom of God.

Therefore, contrary to living in sin, a Christian should highly value themselves, recognizing their own worth as something precious and of inestimable value: for they are a king, priest, and prophet, a child and heir of God. Thus, they should walk and live according to the Spirit, whose fruits are love, joy, peace, patience, kindness, goodness, faith, gentleness, self-control, forbearance, modesty, and chastity. As the same apostle says, there is no law against such things, for they are a law unto themselves. Therefore, there is no condemnation for them, for they are in Jesus Christ, and being in Him, they do not walk according to the flesh, but according to the Spirit. For the law of the Spirit of life in Christ Jesus has set them free from the law of sin and death; and the rest that Paul discusses in this regard in Romans 8:1.

Since all of this we have and are through Christ, it is reasonable for the strengthening of your faith, especially living among infidels and enemies of the cross of Christ (in which the Christian glories), with whom you will have daily conflicts, to discuss what you should believe concerning Christ, in whose name you are called Christians.

Christians must firmly believe, and for this faith, they would lay down a hundred thousand lives if they had them, in one God, the creator of heaven and earth, and that this one God, as He Himself has declared in His Holy Scripture, is Father, Son, and Holy Spirit. The Lord says, "Go therefore and make disciples of all the nations, baptizing them in the name of the Father and of the Son and of the Holy Spirit," Matthew 28:19. And His beloved disciple says, "For there are three that bear witness in heaven: the Father, the Word, and the Holy Spirit; and these three are one," 1 John 5:7-8. This mystery of the Holy Trinity was not left unrevealed to the holy patriarchs and prophets of the Old Testament. True, it was not as clearly revealed as in the New Testament. To confirm this, I will cite only two passages: the first is from Psalm 110, and I will cite it according to the Spanish translation made by the Jews, so they cannot say that our Christian translation is incorrect. "The Lord (*Adonai*, which is the LORD; the Jews, out of superstition, do not want to name Him) said to my Lord: 'Sit at My right hand, Until I make Your enemies Your footstool.'" David, inspired by the Spirit, prophesies in this Psalm of the Messiah, whom we call Christ, two things: first, the offices that the eternal Father would entrust to Him; second, how Christ would conduct Himself in the execution of these offices mentioned here.

The offices mentioned in Psalm 110 are two: His eternal kingdom, which is discussed in the first three verses, and His eternal priesthood, discussed in verse 4. The execution of these two offices is addressed in the rest of the Psalm. This Psalm is of great significance for convincing the Jews about the eternity and divinity of the Messiah, and because of its importance, the Lord, while teaching in the temple, used it for this purpose, as recounted in Matthew 22:42-45. He asked them: "What do you think about the Christ? Whose son is He?" They said to Him, "The son of David." He said to them, "How then does David in the Spirit call Him 'Lord,' saying: 'The Lord said to my Lord, Sit at My right hand, Till I make Your enemies Your footstool'? If David then calls Him 'Lord,' how is He his son?"

These words were so powerful and conclusive that the Pharisees, despite being sophists, cunning, and slanderous, had no answer, and they became so fearful of Him that from then on (as the Evangelist says) they never again came to Him with questions as they used to in order to tempt Him. Thus, leaving behind disputes, they plotted to kill Him; as they indeed did.

David speaks of two persons in Psalm 110: the eternal Father and His Messiah, whom David calls Lord. By calling Him Lord, David indicates that the Messiah is more than a man; He is eternal, He is God. David confirms this with the words the Father says to the Messiah: "Sit at My right hand." To whom, not among men, but even among angels, who are the most excellent creatures, has God ever said: "Sit at My right hand, until I make Your enemies Your footstool"? The apostle, in Hebrews 1:13, uses this statement among other reasons to prove the divinity of the Son of God, emphasizing that God has never said this to any of the angels.

Also noteworthy is what David says in verse 4: "The Lord has sworn and will not change His mind: 'You are a priest forever, in the order of Melchizedek.'" This Adonai, to whom the LORD speaks, this Messiah, this one whom David calls Lord, David himself says will be a priest forever, meaning an eternal priest, in the manner of Melchizedek, not according to the order of Aaron. This implies that with the coming of the Messiah, the priesthood of Aaron, with all its rituals and external worship, would cease, as it indeed did. There would be another priesthood that would never cease but would be eternal, whose priest would also be eternal and not mortal.

Therefore, with the Messiah being an eternal king and eternal priest, and sitting at the right hand of the LORD, as David says in this Psalm, it follows that the Messiah, in addition to being a true man, had to be true God. And this is how the ancient Jews expected the Messiah.

Modern Jews, who have written after the coming of Christ, prefer to avoid any interpretation that aligns with our understanding of Christ. Therefore, some of them interpret the "Lord" mentioned by David in this psalm as referring to Abraham, others to David himself. However, this cannot be true. As for David, he himself calls this Lord his Lord, and neither David nor Abraham were priests, neither in the order of Aaron nor that of Melchizedek. Furthermore, God never told either of them, no matter how holy they were, to sit at His right hand, which would be to confer upon them divine majesty in addition to their human nature, as is true for the real Messiah, our Christ, who is both true God and true man. Thus, Christ is seated at the right hand of the Father, to whom the Father has given all authority, as the Lord Himself says in Matthew 28:18, "All authority has been given to Me in heaven and on earth."

This explanation pertains to the interpretation of the Psalm.

In Isaiah 61:1, it states, "The Spirit of the Lord God is upon me," indicating the presence of all three persons: the Spirit, the LORD (Yahweh), and the one upon whom the Spirit rested, which is Christ. The actions described in this passage, performed by the one upon whom the Spirit of the LORD rested, can be found in no one else but Christ. While all other prophets received the Spirit in measure, Christ received the fullness of the Spirit with all its gifts, without measure. Thus, He alone, with the power of His Spirit, accomplishes everything mentioned here. He is anointed to bring good news to the poor, sent by the Father to heal the brokenhearted, to proclaim liberty to the captives, and recovery of sight to the blind, etc., as the Lord Himself testifies in Luke 4:18, declaring that this Scripture was fulfilled in the hearing of those present.

1.5 Our Scriptural Creed

What we should believe about the Father, the Son, and the Holy Spirit is summarized in the brief confession of faith that all Christians make, known as the Creed, and in more detail in the Nicene Creed and even more expansively in the

Athanasian Creed, which begins with: "Whoever wishes to be saved, etc." Christians should learn from these three creeds what they are to believe about these three persons. In doing so, they will be able to give an account of their faith and will not just be Christians in name or because their parents were, but in deed and truth. They will not be among those who merely say, "I believe in God," or "I believe what the Church believes," without knowing what the Church believes. In this regard, the devil has a great advantage; if asked and willing to respond, he would know much better than them what the Church of Jesus Christ believes.

This Messiah, this Son of God and Redeemer of the world, was promised in the time of the law known as the law of nature and later during the time of the written law. The first promise was made right after Adam's sin, as recorded in Genesis 3. When God questioned Adam about his sin, and Adam blamed his wife, and the wife blamed the serpent, God began His judgment with the serpent. Among other things, He said to the serpent: "I will put enmity between you and the woman, and between your seed and her seed; He (referring to the seed of the woman, which is Christ) shall bruise your head, and you shall bruise His heel." Just as the devil, through his malice, used the woman Eve as an instrument to make Adam and all his posterity sin in him (in whom, says Saint Paul in Romans 5:12, all sinned), so God, in His infinite goodness, used another woman, the Blessed Virgin, from whom the Redeemer of the world was born. This Redeemer would destroy the works of the devil and restore Adam and his posterity to the grace and favor of the eternal Father as before, and even more than before. These, of whom Moses speaks, are the first we read about in Holy Scripture who sinned, and each sinned to a different degree. The serpent or devil sinned out of malice, hatred for the human race, and pleasure in offending its Creator, never repenting. Thus, it sinned against the Holy Spirit, to whom love and charity are attributed, and therefore there was no remedy for its sin. As the Lord says in Matthew 12:32 and Mark 3:29, the sin against the Holy Spirit will never be forgiven. The Pharisees, against whom Christ speaks in these passages from Matthew and Mark, committed this kind of sin.

Indeed, the woman, Eve, deceived by the serpent, sinned due to ignorance. Thus, her sin was against the Son, to whom wisdom is attributed, as He is the wisdom of the Father. Consequently,

Eve, having sinned through ignorance, received forgiveness. Saint Paul, before his conversion, committed this type of sin and was shown mercy, as he himself testifies in 1 Timothy 1:13.

Adam did not sin out of malice like the serpent, nor was he deceived like Eve, but he sinned out of weakness by yielding to eat the fruit that God had forbidden, in order to please his wife. As Saint Paul states in 1 Timothy 2:14, "Adam was not deceived, but the woman being deceived, fell into transgression." This type of sin, a sin of weakness, is against the Father, to whom omnipotence is attributed, and there is forgiveness for it.

This understanding points to the different natures of sin and the corresponding aspects of the Holy Trinity against whom these sins are committed, highlighting the depth and complexity of divine forgiveness and redemption.

Indeed, all sins committed against the divine Majesty can be categorized into one of these three types: sins of malice, ignorance, or weakness.

This same promise, first given to Adam, was reaffirmed to Abraham, Isaac, and Jacob, as recorded in Genesis chapters 23, 26, and 28, respectively. God told each of these patriarchs, "In your seed, all the nations of the earth shall be blessed." This promise was also made to David, and it was a source of consolation for him and other faithful individuals during their times of sorrow and hardship. They firmly believed that God would fulfill His promise and send a Redeemer to deliver them not from the physical captivities of Egypt, Babylon, or Roman rule, but from the spiritual captivity of the true Pharaoh, the true Nebuchadnezzar, the true Antichrist.

God did not just promise the Messiah, but also gave an indication of the time of His coming, the circumstances, how He would come, and the purpose of His coming. This was so that when they saw everything fulfilled, they would be certain that the Messiah had indeed come. Jacob, inspired by the Divine Spirit, prophesied about the Messiah, saying, "The scepter shall not depart from Judah, nor a lawgiver from between his feet, until Shiloh comes, and to Him shall be the obedience of the peoples." This is a particularly comforting and instructive passage in Scripture, speaking so clearly about the coming of Christ, whose kingdom is eternal and whose power is infinite.

However, it's also a passage that the Jews, especially in modern times, have variously interpreted or even corrupted with their fantasies and imaginings due to their animosity towards Christ. While the ancient Jews acknowledged this passage as referring to the Messiah, as does the revered Chaldean paraphrase, which translates "until Shiloh comes" as "until the Messiah comes," modern interpretations vary widely. When they find themselves at a loss for an explanation, they might resort to responses like one given by a distinguished elderly Portuguese Jewish doctor I spoke with. He claimed that Jacob was drunk when he said this and that the Spirit of God had departed from him for attempting to speak of things God had not revealed to him. Thus, Jacob prophesied that descendants of David would govern and rule the Jewish people until the coming of the Messiah, and once the Messiah arrived, He would be the governor, captain, and king.

The Jewish people, scattered around the world for over 1500 years, subject to foreign nations, and often afflicted and mistreated by them, have not had a king or governor from the descendants of David during all this time. They no longer have their great and high priest, who was a figure of Christ, nor do they celebrate the Pesach, the Passover lamb, nor do they perform the other sacrifices of bulls and rams, etc., which symbolized the true sacrifice offered by

Jesus Christ. Where is the Ark of the Covenant? Where are the two tablets on which God wrote the Ten Commandments? Where is Aaron's rod that budded? Where is the golden jar that held the manna? All these have ceased to exist for over 1500 years, and their fate remains unknown.

The prophet Hosea, in chapter 3, verse 4, says: "For the children of Israel shall abide many days without king or prince, without sacrifice or pillar, without ephod or household gods. Afterward the children of Israel shall return and seek the Lord their God, and David their king, and they shall come in fear to the Lord and to his goodness in the latter days." The reference to seeking "David their king" cannot mean David himself, who died over two thousand years ago, but rather Christ. Thus, the Chaldean paraphrase interprets this as: "And they shall obey their king, the Messiah, the son of David." This prophecy about the conversion of the Jews is being fulfilled day by day in those who convert from Judaism, believing that the Messiah has already come.

In Daniel chapter 9, verse 24, a timeline is given for the coming of the Messiah, specified as seventy weeks of years, amounting to 490 years. Daniel states: "Seventy weeks are decreed about your people and your holy city, to finish the transgression, to put an end to sin, to atone for iniquity, to bring in everlasting righteousness, to seal both vision and prophet, and to anoint a most holy place." And in verse 26, he mentions: "After the sixty-two weeks, (to which seven weeks are added as stated in the preceding verse), the Messiah will be killed" (or as the Jewish translation puts it: 'the anointed one shall be cut off'), which means the same thing. Thus, nearly at the end of the seventy weeks, Christ was crucified. Forty years after His death, the Romans, referred to by Daniel as the prince's people, destroyed the city of Jerusalem and the temple, as prophesied in verse 27.

God set a term of seventy weeks, or 490 years, and not only have these 490 years passed, but more than a thousand years have elapsed. Therefore, as the word of God cannot fail, it follows that the Messiah has long since come. Moreover, all the events Daniel said would occur in the first seven weeks, the sixty-two weeks, and the last week, which together make seventy weeks, have been fulfilled. Why then would the prophecy about the coming of the Messiah or the Anointed One not be fulfilled?

God revealed to Jeremiah that His people would be in captivity in Babylon for seventy years.

And as God promised, so He fulfilled it. After the seventy years, He sent Cyrus, who liberated them from temporal captivity. These seventy years were a figure of the seventy weeks Daniel speaks of, and the temporal captivity under the king of Babylon was a figure of the spiritual captivity under the prince of this world, which is the devil. And Cyrus, who freed them from that temporal captivity, was a figure of the Messiah, whom we call Christ, who freed us from spiritual captivity. For there is no other mediator to appease the wrath of God but Him, as the prophets, especially Isaiah in chapter 53, say.

May God have mercy on the poor Jews and grant them grace to turn to Him, to serve the LORD with fear, and to kiss the Son, that is, to give obedience to the Messiah. For if they do not do this, God will become completely angry with them and will destroy them completely, both in body and soul.

To learn about the immense slaughter of thousands upon thousands of Jews, their severe hardships and calamities endured during the siege, and when the city was captured, including the extreme famine to the extent that mothers ate their own children, one can read Josephus' account in *The Jewish War*. Josephus, who was present during these events, details the punishments God inflicted on the Jews for their role in the ignominious death of the Messiah.

The dishonorable death of the Messiah was not first prophesied by Daniel. Isaiah, many years earlier, had foretold it. His Chapter 53 is the most explicit in all of Scripture about the Lord's ignominious death, His victory and triumph over death, and the great benefits humanity received through His death. Isaiah speaks so clearly about these events that, as Saint Jerome notes, it seems less like a prophecy of what was to be and more like an account of what had already occurred.

Two main points can be drawn from this chapter: firstly, the Messiah, to whom the chapter refers (as understood by the ancient Jewish commentators), is truly human. He is whipped, wounded, humiliated by God, killed, and "cut off from the land of the living," with the reason being "the transgression of my people," as mentioned in verses 4 and 8. Secondly, His divinity is evidenced by the statement that He committed no sin and no deceit was found in His mouth. What man does not sin? Solomon says in Proverbs 24:16 that "a righteous man falls seven times, and rises again," implying that even the just sin frequently. And if the just fall often, what of the unjust? They are in constant fall, for whatever man does without faith is sin.

The third aspect of the Messiah's mission is to remove sins by making atonement for them, a task that no mere man can accomplish. Only God can remove, forgive, and blot out sins, as He Himself testifies in Isaiah 43:11: "I, even I, am the Lord; and apart from me there is no savior." Furthermore, Isaiah states that when the Messiah offers His life as an atonement, He will see His offspring, live long days, and the will of the Lord will prosper in His hand. Christ died, but His death was such that death could not hold Him; by His divine power, He resurrected, triumphing over death, sin, and Satan. And all this was for our sake, to obtain forgiveness for us and to reconcile us with His Father, making us His children; and if children, then heirs.

Who can justify men through faith in Him, which the prophet refers to as His knowledge, but God alone? Christ does this, as testified in verse 11, which leads to the conclusion that He is God. We have seen from Genesis 3 that the Messiah was to be the seed of a woman, that is, born of a woman, truly human. His mode of conception and birth is declared by the prophet Isaiah in 7:14, saying, "The virgin will conceive and give birth to a son, and will call him Emmanuel." His most holy mother, a virgin, conceived Him and remained a virgin at His birth. This is the sign that God gives, and the miracle He performs, that a virgin, contrary to the natural course of women, conceives and gives birth. The Hebrew term "*almah*" properly means a *young maiden*, a virgin, as noted by Saint Jerome, which was the case with the Holy Virgin Mary, and with Rebekah in Genesis 24:43, and with Miriam, Moses' sister, in Exodus 2:8.

The place of His birth, prophesied by Micah in 5:2, states: "But you, Bethlehem Ephrathah, though you are small among the clans of Judah, out of you will come for me one who will be ruler over Israel, whose origins are from of old, from ancient times." This passage is remarkable because it confirms both the human and divine natures of the Messiah. His human nature is indicated by His birth in Bethlehem, while His divine nature is referenced by His "origins... from ancient times," meaning He did not begin to exist at His birth in Bethlehem but has existed from eternity. Thus, He is God. Rabbi Solomon acknowledges that the prophet speaks here of the Messiah, the son of David. The scribes, when asked by Herod where the Messiah was to be born, as Matthew 2 testifies, answered: in Bethlehem, citing this passage from Micah as confirmation.

In Ezra 3:12, it is recounted that when the elders, who had returned from Babylon, saw the new temple built by Zerubbabel, and remembered the first temple built by Solomon that the Chaldeans had destroyed, they wept and sighed, seeing that the second temple could not compare to the first in terms of construction, ornamentation, riches, or the abundance of sacrifices. To console these elders, the prophet Haggai in chapter 2:9 told them: "The glory of this present house will be greater than the glory of the former house," a statement confirmed by saying that the Lord Almighty had spoken it. This prophecy was fulfilled when the Holy Virgin presented Christ in the temple and when He Himself entered the temple many times, preached in it, and performed many miracles. The activities that Christ was to engage in during His life were predicted by Isaiah in chapter 61.

Isaiah says, "The Spirit of the Sovereign Lord is on me, because the Lord has anointed me to proclaim good news to the poor. He has sent me to bind up the brokenhearted, to proclaim freedom for the captives and release from darkness for the prisoners," among other things. When coming to Jerusalem to die for the redemption of mankind, and being near Jerusalem, He sent two of his disciples to bring him a donkey and a colt. The disciples, as narrated by Saint Matthew in chapter 21, placed their cloaks on them and had Jesus sit on them, alternating between the two. Many people spread their cloaks on the road, while others cut branches from the trees and spread them on the road. The crowds that went ahead of Him and those that followed shouted, "Hosanna to the Son of David! Blessed is he who comes in the name of the Lord! Hosanna in the highest heaven!"

The manner of Christ's entry into Jerusalem, riding on a donkey and not in a triumphal chariot, yet still received as a prince and king with such solemnity, was not a coincidence. The Evangelist notes that all this was done to fulfill what had been spoken by the prophet: "Say to Daughter Zion, 'See, your king comes to you, gentle and riding on a donkey, and on a colt, the foal of a donkey.'" This is a reference to Zechariah 9:9. Similarly, it was no coincidence that Christ was betrayed for thirty pieces of silver and that Judas, who betrayed Him, in remorse threw the thirty pieces of silver in the temple; this was as prophesied by Zechariah in chapter 11, verse 12: "They paid me thirty pieces of silver as my wages, and I threw them into the house of the Lord to the potter," as cited by Saint Matthew in chapter 27, verse 9.

In keeping with the idea of Christ being sold for thirty pieces of silver, it is recounted in historical accounts that, among other punishments meted out to the Jews, thirty of them were sold for a single piece of silver, with a significant number of these events occurring in Spain. Also, it was not by chance that when Christ was arrested, His disciples deserted Him, as prophesied by Zechariah in chapter 13, verse 7: "Strike the shepherd, and the sheep will be scattered," which is referenced by Saint Matthew in chapter 26, verse 31. Additionally, Christ being lifted up on the cross so that all who looked upon Him, believing in Him, might be saved, was prefigured by the bronze serpent that Moses raised in the desert. In Numbers 21:9, it is described that after the people sinned, God sent venomous snakes among them, which bit and killed many. The people then confessed their sin and asked Moses to pray to God on their behalf. In response, God instructed Moses to make a bronze snake and set it on a pole so that anyone who was bitten could look at it and live. This event was used by Jesus to signify the manner of His death, as He stated in John 3:14: "Just as Moses lifted up the snake in the wilderness, so the

Son of Man must be lifted up, that everyone who believes may have eternal life in Him."

It was no coincidence that His hands and feet were nailed, as David prophesied in Psalm 22: "they pierced my hands and my feet." Modern Jews, in their disdain for Christ, have altered this passage. Instead of reading the Hebrew word "*karah*" (meaning "pierced"), they read "*kaari*", meaning "like a lion." This change follows the Spanish translation used by Jews, but older manuscripts read "*karah*," indicating "pierced." This is supported by the Septuagint, the Greek translation of the Hebrew Bible, and the Chaldean and Ethiopian translations, which also say "pierced." The Masoretes, authoritative Jewish scholars, confirm this reading, as noted by Tremellius and others.

Furthermore, it was no accident that Christ was given vinegar to drink. David had prophesied this in Psalm 69:21, saying, "They put gall in my food and gave me vinegar for my thirst." John 19:28 recounts Christ saying, "I am thirsty", to fulfill this Scripture. Likewise, it was no accident that after crucifying Jesus, the soldiers divided His garments into four parts, but did not tear His seamless tunic, instead casting lots for it, fulfilling the prophecy in Psalm 22:18 as stated by Saint John, chapter 19, verse 24.

Nor was it accidental that the soldiers did not break Christ's legs, as they did with the two thieves crucified with Him. Instead, a soldier pierced His side. John 19:36 states this happened to fulfill the Scripture: "Not one of his bones will be broken."

God commanded in Exodus 12:46 and Numbers 9:12 that when the people of Israel ate the Passover lamb, they should not break any of its bones. Jesus Christ, as the true Passover lamb who takes away the sins of the world, fulfilled this figure of the lamb they ate. Without realizing its significance, the soldiers did not break any of His bones. When a soldier pierced His side with a spear, John states that the Scripture was fulfilled: "They will look on the one they have pierced" (Zechariah 12:10). The apostle, in Hebrews 13:11, finds great significance in the fact that Christ suffered outside the city gate, saying: 'The high priest carries the blood of animals into the Most Holy Place as a sin offering, but the bodies are burned outside the camp. And so Jesus also suffered outside the city gate to make the people holy through his own blood."

It is noteworthy to consider God's judgment, as the Jews killed Christ on the eve of Passover.

Accordingly, God ordained that Vespasian and his son Titus would besiege Jerusalem on the same day of Passover. As a punishment for their contempt of the doctrine Christ preached to them for three and a half years, God decreed they should be besieged for the same period. After which, Jerusalem was captured, leading to an enormous death toll. Josephus, as an eyewitness, reports that the number of dead reached eleven times one hundred thousand.

Almost all the prophets' testimonies we've cited so far concern the suffering, passion, and death of Christ. In all these aspects, if carefully considered, he not only proved to be a true man but, more astonishingly, a true God. As a man, he was born of a woman, but more than a man, he was born of a virgin. As a man, he experienced hunger, thirst, fatigue, and other miseries to which humans are subject due to sin. However, as more than a man, he endured all these free from sin and, by his divine word, healed all kinds of ailments, both physical and spiritual. As a man, he died, but as God, he resurrected himself and others. This aligns with his earlier declaration (John 10:18): "No one takes it from me, but I lay it down of my own accord. I have authority to lay it down and authority to take it up again."

Now, let's demonstrate that what occurred in terms of his exaltation, such as his glorious resurrection and ascension, was also revealed by God to his holy prophets. Saint Peter, in his profound first sermon after visibly receiving the Holy Spirit, stated among other things (Acts 2:30): "Being therefore a prophet, and knowing that God had sworn with an oath to him that he would set one of his descendants on his throne, he foresaw and spoke about the resurrection of the Christ, that he was not abandoned to Hades, nor did his flesh see corruption" (Psalm 16:10). Jonah's three days and nights in the belly of the whale were a shadow of Christ's time in the tomb. Jesus himself said (Matthew 12:40), "For as Jonah was three days and three nights in the belly of a great fish, so will the Son of Man be three days and three nights in the heart of the earth."

David's words (Psalm 68:18), "You ascended on high, leading a host of captives in your train and receiving gifts among men," are applied by Saint Paul (Ephesians 4:8) to Christ's ascension. When the apostles spoke in various tongues on the day of Pentecost, as recounted by Saint Luke (Acts 2), the listeners were divided—some marveled, while others mocked, suggesting the apostles were drunk. To these skeptics, Saint Peter responded not with insults but with gentle clarity, "Men of Judea and all who dwell in Jerusalem, let this be known to you, and heed my words. For these people are not drunk, as you suppose, since it is only the third hour of the day. But this is what was spoken by the prophet Joel...", etc.

1.6 Concerning Jewish Expectations

To confirm our Christian faith and respond to those Jews who mock our Christ and us for proclaiming that the Messiah has come, we conclude that Christ, the Anointed One, is indeed the true Messiah promised by God to the forefathers and foretold by the holy prophets, inspired by the Holy Spirit, long before His coming. In Christ alone, and in no other, do we find the fulfillment of all the prophetic attributes attributed to the Messiah. These include His conception and birth from a virgin prophesied by Isaiah; His birth in Bethlehem as foretold by Micah; His presence in the second temple, making it more glorious than the first as Haggai predicted; His healing not only of physical ailments but also of spiritual ones, requiring divine power, as Isaiah foretold; His entry into Jerusalem riding on a donkey, as Zechariah said; His abandonment by His disciples, also mentioned by Zechariah; His betrayal for thirty pieces of silver, as foreseen by Zechariah; His crucifixion, prefigured by Moses; His hands and feet being pierced, prophesied by David; being given vinegar to drink, again foreseen by David; the casting of lots for His garments, predicted by David; His bones not being broken, as Moses indicated; His side being pierced, as Zechariah envisioned; His death outside the city gate, foretold by Moses; His shameful death and passion, as Isaiah described; His three days and nights in the tomb, signified by Jonah; His resurrection, foretold by David; His ascension, again by David; and the coming of the Holy Spirit, as Joel prophesied.

Besides these definitive signs, the time God promised for the Messiah's coming has long passed. Not only have the seventy weeks of Daniel, which are 490 years, elapsed, but more than two thousand years have passed since Daniel's prophecy. Furthermore, the Jews have not had a king or ruler descended from David, nor a high priest, nor sacrifices, nor any of the other aspects we have mentioned, for many years, as prophesied by Jacob and Hosea. It is, therefore, a pity to see the Jews, who were once the true people of God, now being the outcasts of the world, a situation brought about by God's just judgment for their disobedience and unbelief in killing the Messiah.

Some Jews, realizing the time when the Messiah was promised had passed, proclaimed themselves as the Messiah, thus deceiving themselves and many others. One such figure was a Jew named *Bencosba* or *Barcosba*, who declared himself the Messiah, attracting many Jews to his cause. Remarkable stories are told about *Barcosba*, who led a revolt of two hundred thousand men against the Romans. In response, the Romans, as previously mentioned, sent Vespasian to quell the rebellion. Forty-eight years after the destruction of Jerusalem, the Jews made Betar their capital city and rallied behind another false Messiah in a rebellion against the Roman Emperor Hadrian's forces, who severely punished them, resulting in many deaths. Fray Alonso Venero, in his *Enchiridion de los tiempos* (folio 106), recounts that during the reign of Theodoric in Spain, which began in 441 AD, a devil in human form convinced the Jews that he was Moses and promised to lead them through the sea to the Promised Land. Believing him, many Jews entered the water, where most drowned, and the survivors converted to Christianity.

Many Jewish rabbis, despite being convinced by the clear testimonies of Scripture, refuse to acknowledge our Christ as the Messiah and resort to their delusions. They agree that the Messiah was born during King Herod's reign but claim he remains hidden due to sins. However, there is no consensus on where he is hidden: some say he is in Zion, among angels; others believe he is beyond the Carpathian Mountains; while others think he wanders the world as a beggar, waiting to reveal himself at God's pleasure. This illustrates how the devil deceives them.

Therefore, we should give thanks to the Lord for His great mercy in revealing His Son, Jesus Christ, to us. Belief in Him brings salvation. May God extend this grace to the Jews and all other peoples and nations who do not yet know Him and therefore blaspheme Him. Recognizing Him, may we all glorify and praise Him in unison, as commanded in Psalm 117: "Praise the Lord, all you nations; extol him, all you peoples. For great is his love toward us, and the faithfulness of the Lord endures forever."

Concluding with the Jews, there is a notable passage in Jeremiah 23:5, which validates all three aspects we seek to prove in Christ: His divinity, humanity, and role. Observing the negligence of bad shepherds towards their rational sheep, and rather the havoc they wreak, God threatens these shepherds with punishment and removal from their office. He promises to replace them with good shepherds who will properly tend to the flock. Most importantly, He promises Christ, who is the shepherd of shepherds. In this passage, God says (and since this passage counters Jewish beliefs, I will quote it according to their translation): "Behold, the days are coming, says the Lord, when I will raise up for David a righteous Branch, and he shall reign as king and deal wisely, and shall execute justice and righteousness in the land. In his days Judah will be saved, and Israel will dwell securely. And this is the name by which he will be called: 'The Lord is our righteousness.'"

Almost verbatim, Jeremiah repeats this in chapter 33:14. Ancient Hebrews understood this passage, rightly, as referring to the Messiah, and thus the Chaldean translation renders "a righteous Branch" as "the righteous Messiah." Given that this passage refers to the Messiah, let's examine what God Himself says about Him. First, He mentions that He will raise up a righteous Branch or offspring for David, indicating the human nature of the Messiah, who, according to the flesh, is called and is a descendant of David. Up to this point, we are in agreement with the Jews.

The second thing God says is that the name by which the Messiah will be called is *Yahweh* (which Jews translate as *Adonai*). The name *Yahweh* unequivocally denotes His divinity; although God has many names, which are in some respects communicated to creatures, this particular name, *Yahweh*, signifies the divine essence, God considered in Himself without any reference to creation. It is God's own name, which no creature, however holy, can be called by any means. This is affirmed in Isaiah 42:8, where God says, "I am Yahweh, that is my name." Therefore, since the Messiah is called Yahweh, it follows that He is truly God.

Jews refer to this name as ineffable and thus never pronounce it, though they write it. When Yahweh is written in the Bible, they read *Adonai*, meaning Lord. The reason for the Jewish superstition of not pronouncing the name Yahweh can be found in the preface to the Spanish Bible. That the Messiah's name is to be Yahweh is also attested by ancient Jews. Rabbi Abba, commenting on Jeremiah's Lamentations, asks what the Messiah's name will be. He responds that His name will be Yahweh, citing Jeremiah chapters 23 and 33. Additionally, a commentary on Psalm 20:1 asks why God calls the Messiah by His name, Yahweh, in contrast to earthly kings who do not share their name with their subjects.

The third aspect God reveals about the Messiah is that He is our righteousness. This is the Messiah's principal role, not just being righteous in Himself, but being our righteousness. He descended from heaven, became human like us (except for sin), was born, lived in this world enduring many hardships, and suffered death to be our righteousness, making us just with His righteousness and reconciling us with the Father. As Paul says in 1 Corinthians 1:30, "Christ Jesus became for us wisdom from God, and righteousness and sanctification and redemption."

My desire for you, my brothers and sisters in captivity, rich in the freedom of the spirit, and other Christians in Barbary dealing with Jews in the Spanish language, is to know how to respond concerning the central article of our Christian faith regarding the person of Jesus Christ, His divine and human natures, and His role. This lengthy discussion is intended to reinforce the Christian's faith and provide ample responses and objections to the Jews. Since we were disputing with Jews who do not accept the New Testament, all our proofs and arguments are taken from the

Old Testament and are cited according to the translation made by Jews into Spanish. Now, leaving aside the Jews, let's speak with Christians.

1.7 The Revelation of the New Testament

Regarding the New Testament, the four Evangelists have clearly and straightforwardly written the story of Christ's life and deeds (albeit very succinctly) because if they were to write down everything the Lord did and said, when would they finish? For this reason, Saint John said, in the last words of his gospel, "There are also many other things which Jesus did; if every one of them were written down, I suppose that the world itself could not contain the books that would be written." I refer you to the story of these Evangelists for further details.

Now, for further confirmation of our faith, I will present five types of arguments or reasons recounted by the Evangelists, especially Saint John, which prove the divinity of our Redeemer, Jesus Christ. The first is the testimony given by the Father about Christ at His baptism and transfiguration. "This is my beloved Son, in whom I am well pleased; listen to Him," He says (Matthew 3:17 and 17:5). The second reason comes from the testimony of John the Baptist (John 1:27).

He says, "This is the one who comes after me, who ranks before me, of whom I am not worthy to untie the sandal strap." In saying "before me," he indicated the divinity of Christ, meaning Christ existed before John the Baptist and even before Abraham, signifying His eternal existence. John the Baptist, pointing to Christ, said, "Behold, the Lamb of God, who takes away the sin of the world" (John 1:29).

The third reason comes from the works and miracles performed by Christ, foretold by the prophets, especially Isaiah in chapters 42 and 61, which we have already mentioned. The Jews are inexcusable for having seen Christ's marvelous works and yet not believing in Him. To convict them, Christ says (John 15:24), "If I had not done among them the works that no one else did, they would not be guilty of sin; but now they have seen and hated both me and my Father." And in John 5:36, Christ says, "The works that I do bear witness about me." In John 10:37-38, He states, "If I am not doing the works of my Father, then do not believe me; but if I do them, even though you do not believe me, believe the works, that you may know and understand that the Father is in me and I am in the Father." And in John 14:11, He asserts, "Believe me that I am in the Father and the Father in me, or else believe on account of the works themselves."

The fourth reason for asserting the divinity of Christ comes from the many testimonies found in the Holy Scriptures. Jesus himself, speaking to the Jews, said, "Search the Scriptures...they bear witness about me" (John 5:39). We have already refuted the Jews regarding their awaited Messiah using notable passages from the Old Testament, such as Psalm 110: "Sit at my right hand..." Now, we will briefly cite evident testimonies from the New Testament, which clearly speak of Christ's divinity. These were used by a Spaniard who argued against Erasmus, mistakenly thinking he was an Arian. The first testimony is the name *Immanuel*, meaning "God with us," given to Christ (Matthew 1:23), taken from Isaiah 7. The second is the Gospel of John, written to prove Christ's divinity, where Christ calls Himself God, leading the Jews to want to stone Him for blasphemy. John begins his Gospel: "In the beginning was the Word, and the Word was with God, and the Word was God..." The third testimony is from Thomas, who called Christ "My Lord and my God" (John 20:28).

Fourth Testimony: Saint Paul, as recorded by Saint Luke in Acts 20:28, while speaking to the elders of Ephesus whom he had sent from Miletus and bidding farewell to them, said among other things: "Therefore, watch over yourselves and the entire flock, in which the Holy Spirit has placed you as bishops to shepherd the Church of God, which he obtained with his blood." The apostle confidently refers to the blood of God, acknowledging the union of Christ's dual natures, as he is referred to as "the Son of Man who is in heaven."

Fifth Testimony: In Romans 9:5, Saint Paul, discussing the Jews, states: "Their ancestors belong to them, and Christ descends from them according to the flesh. He is God over all things, blessed forever."

Sixth Testimony: In Philippians 2:6, Saint Paul, speaking of Christ, says: "He, being in the form of God, did not consider equality with God something to be grasped." This statement implies that Christ, being in God's substance as articulated by Athanasius, did not regard his equality with God as something to be exploited. Additionally, Paul elsewhere proclaimed, "I am who I am."

Seventh Testimony: Saint Paul, in Colossians 2:9, speaking about Christ, says, "In him dwells all the fullness of the Godhead bodily."

Eighth Testimony: Saint Paul, speaking to his disciple Titus in Titus 2:11-13, states, "The grace of our Savior God has appeared to all men, teaching us to renounce ungodliness and worldly desires, and to live temperately, justly, and godly in this present age, while we wait for the blessed hope and the glorious appearing of our great God and Savior, Jesus Christ."

Ninth Testimony: The Apostle, in Hebrews 1:8, speaking of Christ, declares, "But to the Son: 'Your throne, O God, is forever and ever.'" Earlier, speaking of the same Christ, he said, "Let all God's angels worship him."

Tenth Testimony: Saint John, in his first epistle, 1 John 5:20, proclaims, "And we are in the true one, in his Son Jesus Christ. *This is the true God and eternal life.*"

The fifth reason is the testimony that Christ gives of himself. Although among men, self-testimony is not considered valid, as civil law states that no one can be a witness in their own case, when the speaker is God, their testimony is valid because God is the truth itself. We have sufficiently proven that Christ is God; therefore, His self-testimony is valid. In John 5:17, Christ tells the Jews, "My Father is working until now, and I am working." The evangelist then mentions that this statement made the Jews more determined to kill him, as they believed Christ not only broke the Sabbath but also called God his Father, making himself equal to God. In John 10:30, Christ says, "I and the Father are one." This statement led the Jews to attempt to stone him, accusing him of blasphemy for, being a man, claiming to be God. Earlier, Christ had spoken about his sheep, saying, "I give them eternal life, and they will never perish, and no one will snatch them out of my hand." Who else but God can give eternal life to those who believe in Him? Thus, Christ, who grants eternal life, is indeed God.

Therefore, having such a great cloud of witnesses placed upon us, including the testimonies of the Father, Saint John the Baptist, the miracles Christ performed, the testimonies from both the New and Old Testaments, and from Christ himself, let us believe with a living faith, grounded in the word of God, that Jesus Christ is true God and true man. He died for our sins and rose again for our justification, as stated in Romans 4:25. This act of salvation is so uniquely Christ's that no one else can perform it. Saint Peter states in Acts 4:12, "There is salvation in no one else, for there is no other name under heaven given among men by which we must be saved." Thus, Christ died to save sinners, of whom each Christian, desiring salvation, must believe they are one. Anyone who does not believe this must understand that they will not be saved but condemned, as our Redeemer himself says to his apostles in Mark 16:16. Saint Paul believed this when speaking to his disciple Timothy, as he said in 1 Timothy 1:15, "The saying is trustworthy and deserving of full acceptance, that Christ Jesus came into the world to save sinners, of whom I am the foremost." Earlier, he had described himself as a blasphemer, a persecutor, and an injurious person. This is what we confess in the creed when we say: I believe in the remission of sins; that is, I believe that although I am unworthy for God to forgive my sins and deserve to be cast into the depths of hell for never having loved Him with all my heart, nor my neighbor as myself, but having broken His law not just once but countless times, I still believe that His Majesty, through His great mercy shown to me in Christ, my Redeemer, which I have grasped by faith, has forgiven all my sins and will not impute them to me. May His Majesty increase our faith; for Satan is very cunning and busy in planting doubts in our minds so that we do not believe we are among those to whom God has forgiven their sins.

The reasons that have moved God to forgive sinners and save them through forgiveness are discussed in various parts of the Holy Scripture. However, here I will mention just one passage that encapsulates all four causes of our salvation. Saint Paul, speaking to the Ephesians in chapter 2, verse 4, says:

> But God, who is rich in mercy, out of the great love with which he loved us, even when we were dead in our trespasses, made us alive together with Christ; by whose grace you are saved. And he raised us up with him and made us sit with him in the heavenly places in Christ Jesus, to show in the coming ages the immeasurable riches of his grace in kindness toward us in Christ Jesus. For by grace you are saved through faith, and this is not from yourselves, it is the gift of God. Not by works, so that no one may boast; for we are his workmanship, created in Christ Jesus for good works, which God prepared beforehand that we should walk in them.

The apostle identifies God's free mercy as the efficient cause of such a great benefit as our salvation; Christ as the material cause; faith as the instrumental cause through which we receive this benefit. Although He died for all, not all will be saved, but only the faithful, only those who believe in Him. The final cause is the glory of God, that we may glorify Him. The Lord, in Mark 5:16, exhorts his apostles to good works, saying: "Let your light so shine before men, that they may see your good works and glorify your Father who is in heaven." We glorify Him when everything we think, say, and do is directed to the glory of God and the benefit of our neighbor. That is why He created us; the good we do for our neighbor, God records in His book of *Account*, God counts it as if it were done to His Majesty. As He himself testifies, saying in Matthew 25:40: "Whatever you did for one of the least of these brothers and sisters of mine, you did for me."

1.8 The Doctrine of Justification

If our opponents, the Catholics, would pay attention to what Saint Paul has done here, which he confirms in many other places, they would not insist so much on saying that a sinner is not justified by faith alone, but that besides faith, good works are also needed for justification. What good works can a sinner, an enemy of God, someone not reconciled with God, not in His grace and favor, do? Everything he does, says, and thinks will be sin; God will abominate it all, because without faith it is impossible to please God, as stated in Hebrews 11:6; and everything not proceeding from faith is sin, according to Romans 14:23. What is the reason that Cain's sacrifice did not please God while Abel's did and was accepted? It's faith, as the apostle testifies in Hebrews 11:4. Thus, it is impossible for someone not justified by faith to do good works that please God. Just as a tree is not good because it bears good fruit, but rather bears good fruit because it is good, similarly, a Christian is not justified before God because he does good works, but rather does good works because he is justified.

Justification causes and produces good works; good works do not cause or produce justification but are fruits of it. A person who does not perform good works should be certain that they are not regenerated, not justified, and do not possess faith; because just as it is impossible for there to be fire without heat, it is equally impossible for someone with true faith, who believes they are justified by the blood of Christ, not to perform good works. Faith without works is not faith, as it is dead. And just as a dead or painted man is not a man but merely an appearance of a man, so too is dead or historical faith not faith, but something that resembles faith. Saint Augustine, among many other statements, says this: Good works follow the justified, they do not precede the one to be justified.

We are not justified by our good works, but by the great mercy of God revealed in Christ, which we grasp through faith. Once we are regenerated and justified by faith, we have peace with God through our Lord Jesus Christ, as Saint Paul states in Romans 5:1. Our actions become pleasing to God, and even though they may contain many imperfections and faults, the Lord does not count these against us. Therefore, we are holy and blessed, in accordance with what Saint Paul also says in Romans 4:7, quoting David: "Blessed are those whose iniquities are forgiven, and whose sins are covered" (Psalm 32:1). The justification of the sinner is not a wage, salary, or payment that God gives to the sinner for their good works, because what good works can a sinner, who is out of favor with God, really do? Justification is an act of God alone, a gift from Him, and a free mercy that He bestows on those He chooses, who are the ones He has eternally elected, predestined, and called to eternal life. To these, He gives true and living faith to make them capable of the promises He makes to them. "All who were appointed for eternal life believed," as Saint Luke states in Acts 13:48. This sound, holy, Christian, and catholic doctrine that a person is justified by faith alone in Jesus Christ, without their works, was preached by the holy apostles, taught by the holy scholars of the Church guided by the Holy Spirit according to what God has declared in His holy Scripture, and confessed by the holy martyrs of Jesus Christ, who were martyred for this confession.

The doctrine that a person is justified by their works, which posits that humans are partners with God and have a role in their own justification, flatters, inflates, and emboldens human pride. By nature, humans are proud, haughty, and arrogant, desiring to be as good and powerful as God Himself. They would, if possible, prefer not to need God at all. This echoes the first lesson taught by the devil when he said, "You will be like gods, knowing good and evil." This notion stuck, imprinted, and deeply rooted itself in human nature—in their understanding and, even more so, in their will. What does an unregenerated person, in their human capacity, desire more than to be a master and to command? Therefore, this new doctrine, concocted by men without the Spirit of God, that it's not enough to believe that Jesus Christ died for our sins and rose again for our justification, but that a person must also help themselves by doing good works, as if the death and passion of the Lord were insufficient for salvation, is particularly appealing.

On the contrary, they condemn, persecute, and burn those who profess and teach the opposite, which is the old and ancient teaching that the prophets, Christ, and his apostles taught and professed. This teaching humbles, confuses, annihilates, and undoes man, giving all glory to God. It sincerely and without pretense acknowledges human misery and inability to do good, and the natural inclination to do evil. It's not surprising to acknowledge this, since Saint Paul, who worked exceptionally hard in converting the Gentiles more than any other apostle and is called the apostle and vessel of choice, confesses this and even more about himself. In Romans 7:15, 19-20, he says, "I do not do the good I want to do, but the evil I hate, that I do. Also, I see another law in my members, warring against the law of my spirit and leading me captive to the law of sin which is in my members." Therefore, he exclaims, "Wretched man that I am! Who will deliver me from this body of death?" And he answers himself: "The grace of God through Jesus Christ, our Lord." Notice, he doesn't say, "I will deliver myself through my good works or my great efforts in preaching the gospel of Jesus Christ, of which I am not ashamed, and for which I am prepared to die, as indeed he did."

It doesn't say, "by my merits, my almsgiving, my fasting, and disciplines," as our modern Pharisees now claim and teach. Rather, it says, "God's grace will save me through Jesus Christ, our Lord." Let us then humble ourselves before the throne of Divine Majesty and with all our heart confess that within us, there is nothing but sins and miseries. If there is any good in us, if we do any good work, if we say or think anything good, it all comes from God. He is the one who enables our understanding and inclines our will so that we can recognize what is good, love it, and put it into action. As Saint Paul says in Philippians 2:13, "It is God who works in you both to will and to do for His good pleasure." And in 2 Corinthians 3:5, he says, "Not that we are sufficient of ourselves to think of anything as being from ourselves, but our sufficiency is from God." Even a regenerated man, like the apostle, cannot of himself think good thoughts. How much less can he speak well or act well? Therefore, give glory to God when doing good and acknowledge our own shortcomings. The question isn't whether we can of ourselves think, speak, or do evil—all this is natural to us because of sin. As God says about man, who He knows well, "Every intent of the thoughts of his heart is only evil continually" (Genesis 6:5). The question is whether a man can of himself think, speak, or do good. The apostle denies this in the previously mentioned passages. Therefore, when we have done good, let us say, as the Lord commanded His apostles to say, "We are unprofitable servants, we have done what was our duty to do" (Luke 17:10). Those who say this are far from thinking that they deserve anything for their works. They are far from believing in works they call 'congruous' and 'supererogatory,' which they don't need and so our adversaries distribute them as they please, engaging in exchanges with them. This doctrine inflates and puffs up man and does not give glory to God; therefore, let us abhor it and embrace the teaching that humbles man and gives glory to God.

Like spiders turn the good juice of flowers, which bees use to make their sweet honey, into poison, in the same way, our adversaries transform this healthy teaching into evil and venom. They claim it is pestilential, heretical, and abominable, and for this reason, they persecute it fiercely and bloodily. They argue that it makes people lazy, lost, and careless about doing good or performing good deeds since they are not saved by these deeds. To this, I respond that there's a difference between asking whether good works justify a person or at least contribute to their justification, and asking whether a Christian, regenerated by the Spirit of God, should and is obliged to do good works, such that if he doesn't do them, he is not a Christian. There's a significant difference between these two questions. Regarding the first, we have sufficiently proven through Holy Scripture that a person, a mortal enemy of God, unregenerated, without the Spirit of God, and without true and living faith in Christ, cannot do anything that pleases God. Without faith, it is impossible to please God. Conversely, everything such a person does becomes sin, because whatever does not proceed from faith is sin. How then can such a person justify themselves before God through their deeds and reconcile with God, becoming a close friend of God, and even more, a child and heir of God? Because all this is included in the meaning of justification.

The answer is clear then: a person in such a state cannot possibly perform deeds by which they are justified and reconciled with God. So, what remedy is there for this miserable sinner? Is there any? I answer that there is none on their part, but there is a unique, excellent, and wonderful one from God. The person will attain it as long as they believe that God is the one who justifies the wicked and that there is no other savior but Him alone, without the company or help of anything else. The way God justifies the ungodly is this: having all humanity turned away from God due to sin and become His enemies, God, moved by infinite mercy and pity, felt compassion for humans. Thus, He selected a good number of them without doing injustice to the others, as they were justly condemned for having turned away from God. Those whom He selected, His Majesty, in His eternal counsel, foreknew and predestined to be made conformable to the image of His Son, so that He might be the firstborn among many brothers. And those whom He predestined, He also called; and those whom He called, He also justified; and those whom He justified, He also glorified, as the apostle says in Romans 8:30.

However, there was a significant obstacle that hindered God's mercy, which was His supreme justice. For God is as merciful as He is just. God had entrusted immense treasures to man, but man, acting deceitfully and irresponsibly, squandered everything and thereby went bankrupt.

God demanded satisfaction; He wanted man to pay back everything owed. However, man was unable to pay, and worse, he detested his creditor so much that even if he had the means to pay, he would not. Then God, being just in all His ways and merciful in all His works, found a way to show mercy to man without compromising His justice. He was fully repaid and did not lose even the smallest amount of what man owed him. The solution was this: God sent His own and only Son, who, by the work of the Holy Spirit, became man in the most sacred womb of the Virgin Mary and was born of her. In becoming man, He did not cease to be God. It was necessary for the redeemer of the human race to be both God and man, for if He were only a man, He would be a sinner like the rest and thus unable to pay or satisfy the Father for our sins; instead, He would need someone to reconcile Him with God. If He were only God and not man, He could not take our sins upon Himself or die for us. Therefore, it was necessary for Him to be both true God and true man, like us in all ways except sin. In this way, He could pay and satisfy for us, which He indeed did, fully satisfying the Father. He took upon Himself the full burden of man's debt, bearing on His shoulders the sins of all humanity.

Therefore, the Son of God, humbled and brought low in this manner, was not spared by the Eternal Father. Instead, He was delivered up for all of us to death, and specifically to death on the cross. This humbling, this obedience, this death on the cross was so pleasing to the Father, so effective and powerful, that the Father considered Himself fully content, satisfied, and completely paid for everything the entire human race owed Him. The certificate and obligation that the Father held against us, which demanded payment of our debt, was torn and nullified, with Christ removing it and nailing it to the cross, as Saint Paul says in Colossians 2:14. Oh, blessed cross! Oh, blessed death and passion of my Redeemer, which brought us so much good! Considering this marvelous benefit that he and all of us received through the death of Christ, the apostle Saint Paul said in Galatians 6:14: "God forbid that I should boast except in the cross of our Lord Jesus Christ, by whom the world has been crucified to me, and I to the world." When Saint Paul speaks of boasting in the cross of Christ, he means that he will only boast in Christ crucified, whom he preached, as he himself says when speaking with the Corinthians in 1 Corinthians 1:23: "We preach Christ cruci-fied, a stumbling block to Jews and foolishness to

Gentiles." The apostle did not glory in the wooden cross on which Jesus Christ was crucified; he did not honor or worship it, as our adversaries command to honor and worship the cross, with the same adoration called *latria*,[4] which is due only to God. I mention this about the cross in passing so that no one should take from this place a pretext for worshiping a wooden or silver cross; for doing so is superstition and idolatry.

Even though the benefit of Christ's sacrifice is offered to all people, and Christ's death is in itself sufficient and adequate to save all who were lost in Adam, not everyone enjoys this benefit. Only those who believe, those who have true and lively faith, which is never idle but works through love, benefit from it. These are the ones who trust in God's word and rely on Him, firmly believing that heaven and earth will fail before God fails to fulfill even the smallest part of what He has promised. This kind of faith is not of our own doing but a gift from God, infused into the hearts of those whom He chooses, a gift of His grace. Hence,

---

4. A theological term used in Catholic theology to mean supreme worship allowed to God alone, a reverence directed only to the Holy Trinity. It carries an emphasis on an internal form of worship instead of external ceremonies which are often empty and void.

the apostle, speaking to the Thessalonians, says, "Not everyone has faith" (2 Thessalonians 3:2). And Saint Luke says, "All who were appointed for eternal life believed" (Acts 13:48). Therefore, my brothers and sisters, let us highly value the faith that our God, moved by mercy and not by our works, has given us. Let us ask Him, as the apostles did, to increase our faith, to make it grow more and more day by day. We see that His Majesty has done this with you. You had some knowledge, a certain awareness and faith in Christ before, but now it has pleased Him to increase it, giving you a much greater understanding of Christ and the benefit of His death and passion. May He who began this good work in you carry it on to completion. Therefore, stand firm in your faith, and as good soldiers of God, resist the enemy in faith. Here, brothers and sisters, we see how God justifies the ungodly by faith, without the help of any good works they might have done or will do. These works do not exist before justification but after, for faith is the root and source from which good works proceed.

Regarding the second question, whether a Christian, regenerated by the Spirit of God, should and is obliged to perform good works, such that if they do not, they are not Christian but hypocritical, I say that such a person is Christian in name only. To better understand this, it's important to recognize that Christian religion consists of two things: faith, by which we are justified before God, and works, through which we obey God, who commands us to do them, and demonstrate to others that we have true faith, and consequently, that we are children of God. The summary of what we should believe is contained, as we have already mentioned, in the creed. The summary of what we should or should not do is contained in the Ten Commandments, which God wrote with His own hand on two stone tablets, as recorded in Exodus 20 and repeated in Deuteronomy 5, where you will find all Ten Commandments complete. Regarding these Ten Commandments, our adversaries, who act treacherously and deceitfully against the God who created them, have completely removed the second commandment, which is against images. Finding themselves with nine commandments, they have split the last one, which prohibits covetousness, into two. Therefore, if we want to be Christians, if we want to fulfill our duty, which is to live according to what God commands us in His law, we need to do what He commands and avoid what He forbids. Otherwise, we will have no part in the kingdom of heaven but in hell. This is why the Lord so emphatically charges us with good works; and this is emphasized in many places in Scripture, of which I will mention some here.

God, speaking to His people in Leviticus 18:5, says: "You shall keep My statutes and My judgments, by which a man may live if he does them." The same is echoed in Ezekiel 20:11 and Deuteronomy 6:5. "We will have righteousness," it says, "when we observe to do all these commandments before the LORD our God, as He has commanded us." The sermons of the prophets are exhortations to keep God's law, to live rightly, and to do good works, with promises from God of all good outcomes and happiness. Conversely, there are threats against all those who do not keep God's law, who live poorly, and who do evil deeds. When a doctor of the law (what we now call a doctor or master in holy theology) asked the Lord what he should do to inherit eternal life, the Lord replied, "What is written in the law? How do you read it?" The doctor answered, "You shall love the Lord your God with all your heart, with all your soul, with all your strength, and with all your understanding; and your neighbor as yourself." To which the Lord said, "You have answered correctly; do this and you will live." Thus, when the Lord on the last day judges all the children of Adam, those who have fed and given drink to the needy, welcomed and cared for the stranger, clothed the naked, and visited the sick and imprisoned, will be placed at His right hand and He will say to them: "Come, you blessed of my Father, inherit the kingdom, etc." Conversely, those who have not engaged in such works of mercy, but have hardened their hearts, not feeding the needy, not welcoming the stranger, etc., the Lord will place at His left hand and say to them: "Depart from me, you cursed, into the eternal fire, etc." (Matthew 25). The apostle Paul, in the epistles he wrote, commonly discusses faith at the beginning, as the foundation and root of the Christian religion, without which faith nothing pleases God. Everything is displeasing to Him, no matter how beautiful it may appear to men, if it is done without faith. The second thing he addresses is works, as the fruits that faith produces.

There are four reasons and motivations for people to do good and avoid evil. The first is necessity; we need to obey God's commandment that tells us to do good and shun evil. The second is the worthiness of good deeds, which please God and are like grateful sacrifices to Him. Consequently,

God honors good deeds with highly honorable titles, while bad deeds receive disgraceful ones. The third reason involves the rewards and punishments that God has promised for good and bad deeds, respectively. This applies not only in this life but also in the life to come. Therefore, if we were at least wise in our own interests and benefit, this should prompt us to do good and avoid evil. The stakes involve either going to enjoy God in the company of angels or going to hell with all the devils. The Lord says in Matthew 25:46, "The wicked will go away into eternal punishment, but the righteous into eternal life."

The fourth reason for doing good works is that they are exercises in which faith is practiced, and they are fruits of the Spirit, just as bad deeds are works of the flesh, of disobedience, and of unbelief. Idleness brings great evils; the devil, seeing someone idle, immediately finds them something to occupy their mind, inundating them with bad thoughts and desires. Once a person conceives sin in this way, they eventually give birth to it. Therefore, a Christian who desires to serve God should engage in acts of faith, in doing, speaking, and thinking good, as this is their duty, for so God commands. Those who understand and hold to what I have said about good works do not belittle them but value them greatly. Thus, they encourage others to do good so that they may be perfect, as their Father in heaven is perfect. Just as it is necessary for the sun to shine, for fire to give heat, and for a good tree to bear good fruit, it is necessary for a Christian to perform good works. May His Majesty increase our faith, so that everything we do may be for His glory.

Despite everything said about the dignity and excellence of good works, that they please God, are a sweet-smelling sacrifice to Him, and are rewarded as such, we must understand that this dignity is not inherent to the works themselves. Even the most perfect good deed we perform is imperfect, tainted, and stained, as Isaiah says in chapter 64, verse 6: "All our righteousnesses are like filthy rags." Therefore, if God were to judge them with the rigor of His justice, He would find plenty of reasons to condemn them. Fearing this, the one whom God found to be after His own heart says in Psalm 143:2, "Do not bring your servant into judgment, for no one living is righteous before you." How then are these works good? How are they pleasing to God? Why does He reward them with life as if they were perfect when they are so imperfect? God does this because of His goodness, not counting their imperfections against them, but accepting and rewarding them as if they were flawless. All of this is because the person performing them is accepted and favored by God, having been justified by faith: "Therefore, since we have been justified by faith," as Saint Paul says in Romans 5:1, "we have peace with God through our Lord Jesus Christ." Therefore, the work pleases God because the person pleases Him, and the person pleases because Christ pleases.

In conclusion, from all that has been said, it is necessary to do good works, and one who does not do them is not a Christian. However, it must also be understood that these good works are neither the cause nor any part of justification; rather, it is the other way around. Justification is the cause and source of all good works. Good works will be the cause or part of justification only when a daughter becomes the mother of her own mother. Therefore, our adversaries are greatly mistaken when they condemn as erroneous, blasphemous, and heretical the proposition that a person is justified by faith and not by works. They not only condemn the proposition but also anyone who upholds and believes it, even resorting to burning them alive, despite God having proclaimed this truth through His holy apostles. Saint Paul, in Romans 3:27, poses the question: "Where, then, is boasting?" The answer: "It is excluded." He asks, "By what law? The law of works?" The answer: "No, but by the law of faith." And in concluding this matter, he states: "Therefore we conclude that a man is justified by faith apart from the deeds of the law." The same apostle reinforces this doctrine at the beginning of chapter 4, saying in verse 2, "If Abraham was justified by works, he has something to boast about, but not before God." (Meaning, he might have reason to boast before men, but not before God.)

Continuing with the Scripture, it states: "Abraham believed God, and it was accounted to him for righteousness." This is explained further: "Now to him who works, the wages are not counted as grace but as debt. But to him who does not work but believes in Him who justifies the ungodly, his faith is accounted for righteousness." This principle is further confirmed by the authority of Psalm 32:1, where David speaks of the blessedness of the man to whom God imputes righteousness apart from works, saying: "Blessed are those whose lawless deeds are forgiven, and whose sins are covered." Just as Abraham was justified by faith and not by works, so too are all those who are justified. They are justified by faith and not by works, as is further elucidated in the subsequent text.

The apostle Paul also cites the example of Abraham in Galatians 3:6 to support his argument that if a person were to be justified by the works commanded in God's law, they would need to perfectly comply with everything the law mandates. For it is written: "Cursed is everyone who does not continue in all things which are written in the book of the law, to do them." This is why James, in chapter 2, verse 10, says: "For whoever shall keep the whole law, and yet stumble in one point, he is guilty of all." It's clear that he refers to the moral law, the Ten Commandments, as he goes on to say: "For He who said, 'Do not commit adultery,' also said, 'Do not murder.' Now if you do not commit adultery, but you do murder, you have become a transgressor of the law." We see that no one, except Christ, has fulfilled everything the law commands with the perfection it demands. Who has loved God with all their heart and their neighbor as themselves? Thus, it logically follows that no one can be justified by works, as no one can perform them as required by the law. Instead, justification comes through the immense mercy of the Eternal Father, manifested in Christ, which we grasp through faith.

The fathers and doctors of the early church held this doctrine to be so true and catholic that they not only said a person is justified by faith but even added, not without scriptural warrant, that they are justified by faith alone. If I were to cite here their notable statements on this matter, it would require many pages. However, to avoid tediousness in a matter so clear and evident, I will only mention a few, as briefly as possible. Before doing so, it's important to note that when the fathers, following the word of God, say a person is justified by faith alone, they mean that justification is solely by God's mercy and solely by the merit of Christ, which we can apprehend with no other instrument than faith alone.

Origen, commenting on Romans 3:27, states: "Justification by faith alone is sufficient so that one, by believing, may be justified even if they have not done any good work." To support his point, he cites the example of the thief who was crucified with Christ and the woman to whom Christ said, "Your faith has saved you." Saint Basil, in his sermon on humility, says: "A person is justified by faith alone." Saint Hilary, commenting on Matthew 8, asserts: "Faith alone justifies." Saint Ambrose, on Romans 3, declares: "Justified freely because, without working or doing anything, they

are justified by faith alone, as a gift from God."
Similarly, on 2 Corinthians 1, he states: "It is
God's ordinance that whoever believes in Christ
is saved without works, freely receiving the remission of sins through faith alone."

Saint John Chrysostom repeatedly affirms in
many places that we are justified by faith alone,
without works. Saint Augustine, who extensively
addressed this topic in his writings against the
Pelagians, whose heresy has been revived by the
Papists, insists that they attribute too much to
man, claiming that he is justified by his free will,
his own strength, and his works. Saint Jerome,
writing to Ctesiphon against these Pelagians and
explaining the apostle's words, "No flesh shall be
justified by the works of the law," clarifies this by
stating that it should not be thought to refer only
to the Mosaic law but to all commandments contained under the name of law. The apostle himself
says, "*I agree that the law is good.*" The examples
cited should suffice.

The Pharisees and hypocrites of our time are
so arrogant, presumptuous, and Pelagian in their
attitude that they are not satisfied with claiming they can fulfill all that God's law demands.
They go even further, asserting that they can and
do much more than what the law requires. This

"much more" they refer to as works of supererogation,[5] which they believe they can grant and apply to whomever they wish, even providing written proof of such. For these individuals, who claim they can fulfill the law and even do more, Christ's death would be in vain. It is certain that if people could do what the law commands with the perfection it requires, they would be justified by their works, and such individuals could be saved without faith, as they would not need Christ. But since no one can fulfill the law perfectly, salvation must come not through works but through faith in Jesus Christ. I challenge these modern Pharisees, these new Pelagians, who so shamelessly claim that they do what God commands and even more, to reflect on when in their lives they have loved God with all their heart and their neighbor as themselves. Their consciences, if not entirely seared and possessed by the devil, will testify that they have never done so as required. They have not loved God and neighbor as they ought; therefore, they are transgressors of the law, they do not fulfill it, nor do they do everything it commands. If they do not do what it commands, much less will they do good that it does not command.

---

5.   The performance of doing more than what is asked for, or more than what duty requires.

The Christian is obliged to do as much good as possible, and even more if they could. Those who have received greater gifts are more obliged to use them well in the service of God and neighbor, for this is the purpose for which God graciously bestowed these gifts upon them. And when a Christian has done all their duty, in accordance with the grace God has given them, they should not become proud, thinking they have done more than required. Instead, recognizing their imperfection and that they have nothing good of themselves, they should give glory to God and acknowledge their own shortcomings. In humility before Divine Majesty, they should say: "I am an unprofitable servant." In doing so, they will highly value the benefit they have received through faith in Christ, who died for our sins and was raised for our justification, and they will strive, with divine assistance, to live their life in such a way (as one who is not ungrateful for such great benefit, grace, and mercy) that God is glorified and their neighbor is helped.

I believe that from what has been said, my brothers and sisters, you will have ample reasons to confirm your faith in Christ against the temptations of the devil, and you will have plenty to answer to Jews and anti-Christians when they ask you about your faith and the hope you have. In this way, you will not be ashamed of the name of Christian that you bear, nor of the Gospel you profess. As Saint Paul said in Romans 1:16, the Gospel "is the power of God for salvation to everyone who believes: first to the Jew, and also to the Greek." Under these two names, Jew and Greek, are included all the nations of the world, which, by believing in the Gospel of Jesus Christ crucified, will be saved, while those who do not believe will be condemned.

1.9 On Witness to Muslims, Jews, and Pagans

To fulfill my promise completely, I must speak about the Moors, among whom you are captives (as it has pleased God, who knows why and for what purpose). When the evangelical doctrine first began to be preached, even while those great preachers, the apostles, the light of the world and salt of the earth as the Lord calls them in Matthew 5, were still alive, significant divisions, schisms, and disputes started to arise in the church of God, even among those who had received the Gospel. I have warned you about this so that you are not scandalized when you see or hear of divisions and sects because of the Gospel.

Among the early controversies was the insistence by many converted Jews (believing that faith in Christ alone was not sufficient for salvation) that Gentile converts to Christ should also observe the Law of Moses, especially circumcision. As Saint Luke recounts in Acts 15:1, they taught the brothers that if they were not circumcised according to the custom of Moses, they could not be saved. To support their false doctrine, they claimed that the apostles in Jerusalem taught this and that Paul, who taught otherwise, was not Christ's apostle but a disciple of Ananias, a disciple of Christ's disciples. Epiphanius notes that one of those who wanted to impose such a yoke on Christians was Cerinthus. Saint Paul vigorously opposed him and others, exhorting the faithful to stand firm in the freedom Christ had given them and not to become again enslaved under a yoke of bondage. He firmly states in his own name that if they are circumcised, Christ will be of no benefit to them. He warns, "Again I declare to every man who lets himself be circumcised that he is obligated to obey the whole law. You who are trying to be justified by the law have been alienated from Christ; you have fallen away from grace. For through the Spirit we eagerly await by faith the righteousness for which we hope."

Saint Paul wrote extensively on this matter in his epistle to the Galatians, many of whom had been misled by false deceivers. The dispute between the two factions became so intense that it was necessary to send representatives from both sides to Jerusalem, where the sacred council of the apostles still resided. Upon arriving in Jerusalem, the apostles and elders gathered to address this issue. The opposing faction had its supporters in the Jerusalem church, including some Pharisees who had become believers. After a great debate, Peter, as one of the principal figures of the council, expressed his opinion. He condemned as an unbearable yoke the teaching of those who advocated for circumcision and adherence to the law as necessary for salvation. He supported and approved the opposing doctrine, the doctrine of faith that Barnabas and Paul preached, concluding his argument by saying: "We believe that we will be saved through the grace of the Lord Jesus, just as they will," referring to both Jews and Gentiles.

The assembly (where each member had expressed their opinion) fell silent to listen to Paul and Barnabas, who were the opposing party. Defending their cause as a principal point of Christian religion, which admits no other righteousness but through faith in Christ, they recounted the great wonders and signs God had performed through them among the Gentiles. After Paul and Barnabas finished speaking, James, acting as the president of the council and reportedly the bishop of Jerusalem where the council was held, heard both sides and, considering the opinions of the council members, resolved the issue on behalf of the church. After endorsing Peter's view, whom he refers to as Simon, and confirming it with what the prophets had said, he concluded: "Therefore I judge that we should not trouble those Gentiles who turn to God, but write to them etc." This decision marked a significant moment in the early church, highlighting the importance of faith and grace over the strict adherence to the Law of Moses for Gentiles converting to Christianity.

The apostles, elders, and the entire church or council then wrote a letter to the Gentile converts. In this letter, they addressed the issue as follows: "Since we have heard that some who went out from us have troubled you with words, unsettling your souls, commanding you to be circumcised and to keep the law, to whom we gave no such commandment, it seemed good to us, having come to one accord, to select men and send them to you with our beloved Barnabas and Paul, men who have risked their lives for the name of our Lord Jesus Christ. Therefore we have sent Judas and Silas, who will also report the same things by word of mouth. For it seemed good to the Holy Spirit and to us to lay upon you no greater burden" etc. Judas and Silas, bearers of the letter, along with Paul and Barnabas, then went to Antioch. Gathering the multitude there, which means the Christian church in Antioch, they delivered the letter. The recipients, upon reading it, were joyful for the consolation it brought, etc.

Here you can see the successful outcome of the question of whether a person is justified by faith without the works commanded by God in His law, in the council that was truly guided by the Holy Spirit. Despite this, the opposing faction did not stop teaching their false doctrine, mixing the law with the Gospel. From these arose the Ebionites and the Cerinthians, from whom later emerged significant heretics like the Arians. The Arians essentially denied our salvation through faith in Christ by depicting Him as lesser than the Father and not of the same substance as the Father. This heresy was condemned in the famous Council of Nicaea, convened by Emperor Constantine. Returning to our main point, about three hundred years after Arius, Muhammad emerged, who composed his Quran or law, mixing elements of Moses' law with the Gospel.

From the law, Muhammad adopted practices like circumcision, abstaining from pork, and ritual purifications including washing. From the Gospel, he borrowed the concept that Christ was the Word of God. He acknowledged that Christ was a spirit, a power, and a soul from God, born of the Virgin Mary, whom she conceived without knowing a man. However, he denied Christ being God or the Son of God, contradicting the clear testimonies from both the New and Old Testaments, which affirm Christ's divinity. Like Arius, he denied that Christ was eternally begotten of the Father's substance. He also denied Christ being a sacrifice for humanity, dismissing much of what the Gospel teaches about the remission of sins and about faith, which receives reconciliation through Christ, the sole mediator between God and mankind. He proclaimed Christ as an excellent prophet and ambassador of God, sent to the world for its improvement. He stated that because people misused Christ's teachings, God sent Muhammad as a more excellent prophet, who would punish with the sword those who did not obey his Quran. Using this doctrine of violence and force, the Muslims conquered Arabia, much of Africa, almost all of the lesser and greater Asia, and a large part of Europe. They were completely driven out of Spain about a hundred years ago. The reign of Muhammad and the papacy began almost a thousand years ago. The first pope was Boniface III; he was the first to call himself the universal bishop, a title none of his predecessors, the bishops of Rome, had ever assumed. Muhammad, around the same time, started his movement with violence, like a lion.

Thus, both have sustained their kingdoms and persecuted the kingdom of Christ; Muhammad with his Quran and the Pope with his decretals. Muhammad commands in his Quran that if any Jew or Christian asks his followers about their law and sect, they should not respond but tell them that each generation is given its law and that everyone should follow their own law. Then they should leave them and not listen to anything further. This error and sect are maintained by Muslims to this day, against all natural reason, which teaches us to seek and love the truth as it comes from God. There is no place where we can find the truth about the knowledge of the true God and the religion and worship with which He wants to be honored, except in the word of God, taught and preached by the holy prophets in the

Old Testament, and Christ and His apostles in the New Testament. If Muslims accepted the sacred Scripture, there could be a debate with them. But since they do not accept it, there is no point in discussing with them; for there is no argument against someone who denies the fundamental principles of religion, which is the word of God. The method of argument they prefer and use is through arms, fire, and blood, not reason. We conclude by saying that it is impossible for a religion that discards the teachings of the prophets and the apostles to be the true religion with which God is served. The Quran rejects the teachings of the prophets and the apostles, so it is not the true religion of God. Furthermore, the true religion is confirmed by the word of God; thus, where there is no word of God, there is no true religion.

May the Lord, in His great mercy, continue the good work He has begun in you, granting you grace to grow daily in faith and in the knowledge of His mercies. May He enable you to progress from virtue to virtue, so that through your exemplary patience in hardships and your kindness and holiness of life, even your adversaries might be inwardly convinced, even if they do not openly admit it, saying: "Certainly, we were mistaken; these people are different from what we thought," etc. It's possible that through your good life, your exemplary piety and kindness, and your reasoned discussions about the things of God, which they will hear and see in you, some of them may turn to the true Christian faith. This is not impossible; there have been instances where, through a single captive, many people and sometimes even entire kingdoms have been converted to our holy Catholic faith, as written in the sacred Scripture. The same can happen now, where God might use you as an instrument to bring about the conversion of some.

Andres Hyperius, a learned and pious man from Flanders, in his first book titled *De Sacrae Scripturae Lectione Quotidiana* (On the Daily Reading of Sacred Scripture), a book certainly worthy of being read, collected some notable examples relevant to this topic. I will use his work here. He describes how, although it has often not been possible for bishops and preachers to enter foreign, barbaric, and remote nations to preach the Gospel, there have been instances where a common man, perhaps a craftsman, soldier, merchant, or agent who was taken captive, ended up among such peoples. Having devoted himself to the reading of the sacred Scripture when he was free, as soon as he acquired some knowledge of the language of the people who held him captive, he began to discuss the principal points of the Christian religion, initially with a few and then, over time, with many. Ultimately, he persisted in doing this with such remarkable spirit, grace, and vehemence that many of his listeners willingly embraced our religion. Thus, those whom neither the care nor diligence of bishops, nor the arms of kings and princes, nor any force, power, or cunning could ever make our friends, were brought to us by a bit of knowledge of the word of God held by a humble layperson. This brought them to us and united us with an indissoluble bond that cannot be broken.

Rufinus, in his Ecclesiastical History (Book 40, Chapter 9), and Theodoret (Book 1, Chapter 22) recount a remarkable story about a young man named Frumentius. Educated in piety and good letters, he traveled to India in the company of Meropius, a philosopher from Tyre. There, Frumentius was captured and made to perform menial tasks. Eventually, he was taken to the court and, excelling in all his duties, was given a position or office. Seizing the opportunity, Frumentius gathered together some Roman merchants who were well-versed in our religion. With their help, he began to form congregations

in the manner of Christians, and with great per-
severance and sincerity, he preached the Gospel
to them. Ultimately, through his exhortation and
the sermons he delivered, he influenced the entire
kingdom to convert to Christianity, leading them
to firmly believe in Jesus Christ as the sole and
unique Redeemer.

The same authors, in the following chapters,
tell of a Christian woman of humble status who
was taken captive in the land of the Iberians, a
northern people. Greatly distressed by the foul-
ness of the dungeon, she devoted herself to fasting
and prayer. She so fervently invoked the Lord that
she soon acquired remarkable and truly apostolic
virtues. First, she was granted the great gift of
performing miracles and wonders. In addition,
she taught the principal points of Christian religion with such grace that it was admired by all
and unmatched by any. Thus adorned with these
gifts, which she exercised with great diligence
and singular faith, she quickly brought the king,
queen, and all their subjects to the knowledge of
the true God and our Savior Jesus Christ. Once
converted, she persuaded them to build tem-
ples for congregating to hear the word of God
and exhorted them to send ambassadors to the
great Constantine, then the emperor of Rome,

to request learned men to teach them. The good emperor was as delighted with this embassy as if he had conquered new kingdoms and provinces with his armies. He promptly sent men of very good and holy doctrine to them.

Nicéforo Callistus also writes in Book 8, Chapter 35 of his Ecclesiastical History about a man named Gregory. Peridates, the king of the Armenians, had imprisoned him in a deep and muddy pit. After enduring many insults, various labors, and torments for fourteen years in that place, Gregory converted the whole of Armenia, leading them away from idolatry to worship the one and eternal God according to the Christian religion. The same author, in Chapter 33, mentions that the wars Romans waged against barbarian nations, especially under Emperor Gallienus and his successors, were often instrumental in spreading and propagating the Christian religion in various parts of the world. This was because the Romans, when captured by barbarians, taught their captors the true Christian religion. Zonaras, a Greek author, recounts that during the time when the Bulgarians were waging a cruel war against the Constantinopolitans, the Constantinopolitans captured a noble maiden who, upon being taken to Constantinople, greatly advanced in good letters and evangelical doctrine. When she returned to her homeland, she persuaded the king of the Bulgarians (who was her brother, unknown to the Constantinopolitans) and his subjects to become Christians. This happened in the year of the Lord 866, etc.

The same God who, through the young Frumentius, a humble woman, Gregory—a despised and downtrodden captive in the eyes of the world, a noble maiden, and other similar means, brought about the conversion not only of individuals but also of kings and entire kingdoms, is the same God who lives and reigns today. He can now accomplish similar feats through any one of you. Therefore, stand firm in your faith; amid your unbearable labors, in your prisons and dungeons, meditate on what you have read or heard from the sacred Scripture. Remember what your Redeemer suffered for you, leaving you an example so that you might also suffer for Him. Resolve in this (which will make your burdens much lighter): what you suffer now for Christ pales in comparison to the coming glory that will be revealed to you through Him. What you are enduring is temporary and will eventually end, but the glory you hope to enjoy, and will enjoy, will be eternal, never to fade away.

Therefore, call upon the Lord to assist you and give you strength, not only to believe in Him but also to suffer steadfastly for His name. It could be that the Lord intends to use you as a means to convert some of those who now persecute you. I will conclude my lengthy discourse with what Saint Paul says in Ephesians 6:5, addressing servants and captives like yourselves. "Servants (or captives)," he says, "obey your earthly masters with respect and fear, and with sincerity of heart, just as you would obey Christ. Do not work only to please men, but as servants of Christ, doing the will of God from your heart. Serve wholeheartedly, as if you were serving the Lord, not people, knowing that whatever good anyone does, this he will receive back from the Lord, whether he is a slave or free."

1.10 Closing Words

My dearly beloved brothers and sisters in the Lord, accept my good intention to do you some good and service. I have done what I could; may His Majesty supplement the rest. Pray to the Father of mercies for His holy, catholic, and apostolic church, that He may preserve and protect it against the tyranny of the papal decretals, the Talmud of the Jews, and the Quran of Muhammad. Pray for our Spain, especially for the king and all those in charge of the republic, that God may grant them the grace to read and meditate on the sacred Scripture, without the knowledge of which it is impossible (as we have sufficiently proven through Scripture and the ancient doctors) for them to fulfill their duty or for the subjects to be well-governed in the true fear of God. Also, pray for me. I am certain that God hears the prayers of captives and the groans and sighs of the afflicted (such as yourselves) when they call on Him with faith and without any doubt. For, as James says in chapter 1, verse 6, "the one who doubts is like a wave of the sea, blown and tossed by the wind. That person should not expect to receive anything from the Lord."

I certainly remember you in my prayers, imploring the Father of mercies to increase your faith, give you patience in your afflictions and captivity, make you steadfast in the confession of His name, and enrich you with His spiritual gifts. So that when the Lord comes to judge the living and the dead, finding you as such because He has made you so, He may say to you: "Come, you blessed of my Father, inherit the kingdom prepared for you from the foundation of the world."

To Him, who with the Father and the Holy Spirit lives and reigns eternally, be glory and honor forever. Amen.

ABOUT THE CÁNTARO INSTITUTE

Inheriting, Informing, Inspiring

The Cántaro Institute is a reformed evangelical organization committed to the advancement of the Christian worldview for the reformation and renewal of the church and culture.

We believe that as the Christian church returns to the fount of Scripture as her ultimate authority for all knowing and living, and wisely applies God's truth to every aspect of life, her missiological activity will result in not only the renewal of the human person but also the reformation of culture, an inevitable result when the true scope and nature of the gospel is made known and applied.